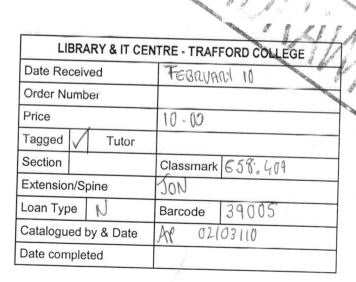

Psychological
Testing
for Managers

Psychological Testing for Managers

A COMPLETE

GUIDE TO USING

AND SURVIVING

19 POPULAR

RECRUITMENT

AND CAREER

DEVELOPMENT

TESTS

Stephanie Jones

PIATKUS

to Yvonne Sarch
friend & collaborator!

© 1993 Dr Stephanie Jones

First published in 1993 by
Judy Piatkus (Publishers) Ltd of
5 Windmill Street, London W1P 1HF
Reprinted 1993

First paperback edition 1993

A catalogue record for this book is
available from the British Library

ISBN 0-7499-1178-6
ISBN 0-7499-1297-9 (pbk)

Edited by Carol Franklin
Designed by Chris Warner

Typeset by Wyvern Typesetting Ltd, Bristol
Printed and bound in Great Britain by
Biddles Ltd, Guildford and King's Lynn

Contents

Acknowledgements

This book would not have been possible without the enthusiasm and co-operation of a number of occupational psychologists, who freely gave of their time in putting me through their tests. (Some even gave me lunch too!) Olya Khaleelee of Pintab was among the first to encourage my interest in this field, by taking me through the DMT, to be followed by the Colour Test, Raven's, and Watson Glaser. She was always happy to provide general advice, books and papers, and offered constant encouragement.

Rob Irving of Whitehead Mann Limited's Audit and Assessment Centre was another keen supporter of the project, and introduced me to a fascinating series of short tests, many of them imported from the USA. Rob also shared with me the model of corporate cultures outlined in the Introduction. Norman Buckley very helpfully explained his Insight Profile system, and provided notes for the background material included below. John Smith, who introduced me to Norman, was another long-term influence on this book, and allowed me to use his in-house SPQR test. At the PA Consulting Group, Caroline Sharley organised for me to experience PAPI, Myers Briggs and 16-PF. At Saville & Holdsworth, Dr George Sik supervised my efforts on the OPQ 4.2, and at Omega, Dr George New and Paula Sprayson spent several hours administering their Motivation and Competency Inventory. Finally, one of the most enjoyable tests of all was the Belbin Team Role Model, for which I am grateful to Jeff Hayden and Nick Lacy-Hulbert.

I would also like to acknowledge the time and efforts of Barry Curnow in providing me with such relevant and thoughtful material, and Yvonne Sarch for her users' insights. Ljilijana Bogdanovic and David Myers helped with the typing, and Gill Cormode was a helpful and encouraging editor.

Preface

The idea behind this book came from my work in researching and writing about various aspects of the corporate human resources world. Over the last few years, I have looked in some detail at executive search and selection, interim management and outplacement, all of which make use of psychological testing as a tool to help match people to particular jobs and career opportunities. Psychological testing is clearly becoming more and more common in the workplace. As a result, I wanted to find out more about it, especially about the different tests, how they are used and what they reveal.

However, all the books that I could find about occupational psychology, and psychological and psychometric testing, were written by professional psychologists, and seemed full of technical jargon and incomprehensible detail. These books were largely about models and theories of personality. They referred occasionally to specific tests, but without explaining what they were like, either from the point of view of the person being tested, or the user of tests.

If you knew you would have to undergo psychological tests in order to be selected for a job, or as part of an appraisal for promotion or transfer, wouldn't you want to know what the tests might entail? If you had not done a test before, you might feel at a disadvantage to someone who had.

Similarly, personnel managers or directors without a background in psychology may be interested in using psychological tests, but have hesitated in the past through lack of knowledge. And many employers know very little about the range of tests available. They either depend on second-hand recommendations or opt for the most commonly used tests without an awareness of the alternatives.

I would like to emphasise that *Psychological Testing for Managers* is absolutely *not* the last word on the subject, but is an introduction for the non-psychologist, both as testee and user. It looks at a range of the most commonly used tests (19 in number) in non-technical language, in a novel format, and explains what the tests involve, when they should be used, and how they can be combined with other tests to give a well-rounded picture of employees' strengths and weaknesses.

I have also tried to give the reader a feel for what it is like to do these tests. To achieve this, I did all the tests myself, and occasionally I explain the nature of the feedback in terms of my own results. After the last test, I was told that I was suffering from test-overload, and that the value of doing any more was now limited! So I would not recommend any individual to do more than a few in close succession.

One of my first experiences of professional writing – more than 10 years ago – was as a restaurant critic, and sometimes I've jokingly referred to this book as 'The Egon Ronay Guide to Psychological Testing'. I certainly hope it will introduce you to the variety and the benefits of psychological testing, whether you are a potential user of tests, or have – or expect to have – experience of them as a candidate for a job or promotion.

If *Psychological Testing for Managers* creates a feeling of familiarity with the concepts, banishes anxiety, allows for critical comparison and provokes interest in the wider subject of occupational psychology, then this book's goals will have been achieved.

CHOOSING THE PSYCHOLOGICAL TESTS FOR THIS BOOK

The tests examined here represent a variety of categories and approaches covering especially intelligence and personality assessments. Among the most established and respected are the Watson Glaser Critical Thinking test, Raven's Progressive Matrices, the Cattell 16-PF and the Myers Briggs Type Indicator. They are still widely used and have many long-term, loyal adherents.

PAPI and OPQ are more recent developments, the latter created by Saville & Holdsworth as a new range of tests for the management market. Their norms are inevitably less extensive, and they have not yet stood the test of time, but they must be welcomed as a major step forward in user-friendliness.

I selected these 19 tests by talking to a number of occupational psychologists, and asking them which ones they thought were most commonly encountered. Each new psychologist I met was asked the same question, and so the list grew and grew. The tests included here are all widely available in the UK, the USA and parts of continental Europe. A number of them, especially the OPQ and PAPI, have been translated into foreign languages. If you think that an especially important or useful test has been left out, please write to me and tell me about it.

Dr Stephanie Jones

Introduction

(Note: the world of psychological testing attributes specific meanings to specific words. Words highlighted in this section, the first time they appear, such as **ABSTRACT**, are explained in the glossary on pages 17–22.)

We all realise that, fundamentally, everyone is different. We all know people who seem to be a world away from ourselves: in their ideas, their appearance and in the way that they go about doing things. It is these differences that make people interesting and that allow us to learn from each other as we go through life. Wouldn't it be boring if everyone was the same?

It is these differences, too, which make it worth while for a person to look for a change in job or career, or for a company or organisation to employ someone new, so that they can bring fresh ideas or a new style of operation to a job. But it is also these differences which may mean that the job or career a person chooses is successful or not, or the person the company or organisation employs is the right person for the job or not.

As journalist Chris Partridge pointed out in an article in the *Observer* of 23 February 1992: 'The risks involved in appointing the wrong person for a job have never been greater. In a recession, only the strongest survive, and companies can no longer afford to carry dead weight. So, it is no surprise that personnel managers turn increasingly to psychology to help them select the person with the right personality for a vacancy.'

Thus **PSYCHOMETRIC** or psychological testing has become a vital tool in the task of minimising risk on all sides in recruitment and in career management decisions. As more and more employers use psychological testing, more and more people in the workplace will find themselves being tested. But which psychological **TEST** or tests should be used, in which circumstances, and why?

'There is a veritable battery of psychometric tests on the market that, the designers claim, provide insights into the mind which can

1

sort the sheep from the goats', Partridge continued. 'They range from full-scale examination of a candidate by a trained psychologist to relatively cheap computerised ones administered by a personnel officer.' As a person being tested (**THE TESTEE**), the range of tests you could face is increasingly large; as an employer (or user), the choice available is also growing all the time.

WHICH TEST?

This book, unlike most other books on psychological testing, lists a series of tests in order to provide you – a person about to undergo psychological testing, or a potential user of tests on your own managers – with a brief introduction to a range of popular tests used frequently in a variety of organisations. It has been written with these scenarios – among others – in mind:

Testee

- You have applied for a job and, at the first interview, you are told that the prospective employer is quite interested in you, but their practice is to put everyone through the Watson Glaser Critical Thinking Analysis. You haven't heard of this and have no idea what it might entail.

- You are approached by a headhunter and agree to discuss a possible job opportunity. The headhunter insists that, in order to go on to the next stage, you must undergo 'a battery of short psychological tests'. You have no clue as to what this means, and you don't know the names of any popular, short psychological tests to ask if these will be included.

- You are being considered for promotion to a different position in the company. It is agreed that you have the qualifications and experience to do the job, but your boss is concerned that you may or may not 'fit in' with the new team. This team has already gone through the 'Belbin Team Roles exercise' and you must go through it too. What is this? Should you be worried about it?

User

- You are the manager of a small, entrepreneurial group developing new products for the parent organisation. You have been asked to recruit two new members of staff, who must be self-starting, creative, risk-taking and decisive. You've heard about the use of psychological tests in selection and feel this could help here. But which test do you use?

- You are the managing director of a well-established, medium-sized company, about to retire after 15 years, having built up the business from a start-up. You have created a group of managers to run the divisions of the business. You would like one of them to succeed you, but which one? Who has the necessary vision and leadership to take over?

- You have just started working in a small recruitment consultancy, and one of the clients asks that all candidates for his assignment should undergo a series of psychological tests. He doesn't know much about these and wants you to advise him. What do you say?

HOW TO USE THE TEST SUMMARIES

This book looks at a range of popular psychological tests, which I have analysed and discussed in such a way as to help you answer the questions above. Other benefits include:

Testee

- If you are told that you are about to be given a certain psychological test, you can read about it and mentally prepare yourself.

- If you are told you are to be presented with a battery of tests, you can quote the names of some of the short tests described here – OPQ, PAPI, Myers Briggs, 16-PF, FIRO-B – and ask if any of these are on the agenda. The odds are that at least one will be. The Saville & Holdsworth OPQ is particularly popular as part of a battery.

User

- If you need to find a certain test or tests which show up specific qualities in individuals, you can look up the descriptions of a number of the tests to see which might be most suitable.

- If you need to recommend the use of specific tests to another person, you can discuss the most popular tests available, how they can be combined and quote the experiences of other users.

PRESENTATION OF TEST SUMMARIES

The tests are presented here in a uniform format to help answer the most commonly asked questions about each test, from the point of view of both the testee and the user.

Background

This describes the origins of the test and examines its usage, popularity and **NORMS**.

The aims of the test

This itemises the aspects of aptitude, **PERSONALITY** and/or ability being tested in each case.

The format

This basically describes what the test looks like, and how it is likely to be presented to you as a testee. The aim is to familiarise you with its format and offset 'fear of the unknown'. For example, is the test **IPSITIVE** or not?

Range of APPLICATIONS

This lists the ways in which the test can be used, particularly in terms of recruitment selection, career development etc., for the user.

Doing the test

This tells you, as the testee, what it's like to actually do each test. It was written immediately after each test was administered to me, and conveys first impressions as well as more detailed reflections and comparisons with other tests.

Examples of content of the test

When there are no copyright restrictions, this section quotes actual extracts from the test. This should serve to overcome a feeling of unfamiliarity with a test. If you have not done tests before, it should help you to gain a certain amount of prior experience. None of these tests are easily available off-the-shelf, and in most cases can only be sold to qualified psychologists.

Time needed to complete the test

This gives an approximate idea of how long most people take to do the test. This is useful when putting together batteries of tests and estimating scheduling times for users, and gives guidelines to those completing the test for the first time.

Time to SCORE the test

This is helpful for the user in choosing tests which are based on speed of obtaining RESULTS. It is particularly necessary to know this if you want a test which can be administered, scored and the results presented to the person being tested on the same occasion. As a testee, can you reasonably expect to be given the results of the test on the spot?

Necessary time for FEEDBACK

This is also useful for an employer or headhunter to know when scheduling a number of people to be tested, and for the person being tested. How long does the entire exercise take? Everyone being tested should insist on feedback, and knowing the average time it takes to receive feedback on a particular test can assure you, as a testee, that you have received more, or less, feedback than usual.

Format/structure of the feedback

This indicates the topics that will generally be covered in the feedback. This is a useful indication of the content of the test, and can help the user to decide if this test is appropriate for a particular use; it also helps you as the testee to know what to expect. If you feel that you are not receiving adequate feedback, then this section helps you to suggest other areas to cover.

Value to the employer/user

This summarises the value of a particular test for the user, in terms of the qualities being tested and occupational applications.

Value to the employee/person being tested

This summarises how the test helps you, as the testee, to understand your qualities in the context of the situation for which you are being tested. If, as an applicant for a job, you are unsuccessful, you should still insist on feedback, so that you can, at least, gain the benefit of having undergone a psychological test which might tell you something new about yourself.

Value to the user organisation

This section in particular looks at the value of the test in determining the suitability of a person for a specific corporate culture. Here, the test will be discussed in terms of how the person will fit into a 'macho' culture, a 'process' culture, a 'retail' culture, and a 'high-risk, slow-feedback' culture (discussed further below).

Can the test results be deliberately falsified?

In most cases, you will find that test results *cannot* be falsified, and even if they can, then the fact that they were will be discovered sooner or later, to the detriment of the relationship between the employer and employee.

Advantages over other tests

This looks at why a particular test is preferred by users and those being tested for certain qualities, including speed of being administered, **VALIDITY**, the extent of validation etc.

Disadvantages compared with other tests

This balances the summary above in terms of the drawbacks of each test. There is certainly no such thing as the 'perfect' test, and this is why combinations of tests can be particularly valuable.

Tests may be combined with...

This suggests combinations of popular tests for specific purposes. Some tests stand up well on their own for a variety of applications, while others are best for confirming or questioning the results of other tests. In most circumstances, especially in recruitment selection, tests will be presented in a group rather than singly.

STATIC/PREDICTIVE value

This indicates the value of the test in describing the attributes of the person being tested at the point in time when the testing exercise takes place, compared with how useful it is in indicating how the person being tested will behave in the future. Different tests have different degrees of usefulness in predicting future behaviour.

Overall review

This summarises the basic features of each test.

How to prepare yourself for sitting this test

This suggests what you should do if you are taking the test for the first time. It cannot tell you how to affect the results of the test to fit in with the impression you want to convey; on the contrary, it warns against attempting this. Instead, it suggests how you should prepare yourself mentally for answering the questions as frankly as possible so that the test can be of the maximum benefit to both parties.

Will this test produce a different result after a period of time?

This section looks at the shelf-life of each test according to the results produced about one individual, suggesting when it could be repeated. It could be that, if you are being tested for a particular job or promotion and you are told which test is being used, you have done that test before. If you did it less than six months before, probably the results are still valid. If it was much more than a year before, then you may well have to retake the test. As a testee, you should always insist on having a copy of your test results in case this happens. It can be useful for employers to know for how long the results of tests are valid when planning career development. Some tests can only be done once, as part of the test is the novelty of the experience of doing them.

The best way of using this book is to derive an overview of the most popular tests, and then look at individual tests in detail on an as-needed basis, either as a testee or user. Further information on particular tests can be obtained from the books listed in the Further Reading list, and by contacting the organisations listed in the Useful Addresses section.

PSYCHOLOGY AT WORK

Management theorists have, for many years, argued that effective management is only possible with a thorough understanding of employees' personalities and behavioural styles, as well as their working situation. Research also shows that a 'person-centred' rather than 'production-centred' management style produces better, and more effective, business results in the long term.

Therefore, in the field of personnel selection, team-building and career development, identifying the way in which an employee differs from others is important. To do this we need 'tools' which will allow us to look at different aspects of personality, and which will give us an indication of how someone is likely to react in certain circumstances, say, if they are under stress, or in a situation which demands a high level of tact and diplomacy. In short, what we need is a model or series of models which can be used to help managers understand their employees better and adjust their management style accordingly.

Personality tests which use sound psychological methods can provide managers with information relating to basic aspects of personality, so that predictions about behaviour can be made with a fair degree of confidence, including **COMPETENCE** and **MOTIVATION**. This information is important when a company or organisation is making decisions about the recruitment, appraisal or development of staff, or needs to form new teams for specific tasks.

Psychology is going to play an ever more important role in the workplace of the future. To be effective, successful and reasonably satisfied in their working environment, managers must be able to come to terms with their own psychology and that of their colleagues. If you are a senior manager, you must be able to use this knowledge and insight to make appropriate hiring and promotion decisions.

Psychological testing will enable you to have some understanding of how you relate to others, and of how others relate to you. The age of the lone-ranger manager is long over, and effectiveness is now about being able to work in teams, in almost every workplace situation.

Essentially, everyone must share the responsibility of living on a small planet with people whose psychology is different from their own. An understanding of psychology and of psychological **PROFILES** should therefore be a vital ingredient in any senior manager's repertoire. This will become increasingly important as the competitive environment facing most organisations becomes more and more sophisticated.

THE THEORIES BEHIND OCCUPATIONAL PSYCHOLOGY

Since the first personality tests were developed, different theories have formed the basis for specific personality tests. Typically, psychological/psychometric models of personality have identified a number of core personality traits, with the number of traits identified by any particular theory varying from 2 to 16, and in a few cases even more.

One of the earliest theories of personality, now very well known and widely adopted, is the two-factor model proposed by H. J. Eysenck in 1947. He argued that the major source of individual personality difference could be reduced to two basic factors, each of which operated independently of the other. The first of these two factors was *Introversion* vs *Extroversion*, and the second, *Stability* vs *Neuroticism*. To a large extent, many personality tests on the market today hinge on these basic findings of Eysenck, which in their turn make use of a number of the findings of Jung and Freud.

So how did early psychologists arrive at their theories of personality? Eysenck, for example, discovered his model by gathering responses to questions about a large number of personality variables. This showed that several apparently different personality traits seemed to cluster together: an individual who scored highly on, say, acting impulsively and risk-taking, would also tend to score highly on sociability and activity. To Eysenck, this implied that there was some common factor underlying these specific personality traits.

Eysenck's model, however, provided only a limited insight into human personality. Many felt that a more sophisticated model was needed, and other researchers began to produce them. This ultimately led to the creation of many of the well-known personality tests on the market today.

WARNINGS FOR POTENTIAL USERS

According to Barry Curnow, a Past President of the Institute of Personnel Management, as the use of psychological testing has become more widespread and users have become more familiar with testing techniques, there has been a growing concern that, instead of using tests as a way of adding value to other management information sources, many users are taking advantage of the availability of test batteries as a quick fix in their human resources decisions. Companies are sometimes using tests as a substitute for management judgement rather than as an aid to such judgement.

It cannot be emphasised too strongly that psychological tests in any form can only aid and inform management judgement; they cannot replace it. Managers are not absolved from making difficult – or easy – selection and/or promotion decisions through the use of psychological tests, however skilfully they are **INTERPRETED**. Psychological tests should never be used as a means of letting managers off the hook.

Barry Curnow always suggests that a battery of tests can be used provided the client is prepared to use them as part of a systematic procedure that includes a number of steps and stages, with built-in checks and balances. The client must take the time to understand the tests and what they attempt to achieve. The client must also be prepared to allocate the time and money for adequate explanation and feedback.

Psychological testing should be seen as part of the wider and continuing process of seeking to understand individuals in the context of career development and team-building, to show strengths and weaknesses, and areas for future attention. They should not be used for selection only, and then put away in the filing cabinet and eventually, inevitably, shredded.

WHAT TESTS SAY ABOUT AN EMPLOYER

It can be revealing for prospective – or existing – employees to examine critically their company's choice and use of psychological tests. Which ones do they prefer? Do they tend to use just one or two, or several? Are they modified or entirely changed from time to time, or is there a long tradition of using only tried and tested **INSTRUMENTS**? Are acceptable and controlled, user-friendly conditions provided for those undergoing the tests? Most important, how much preliminary information and post-test feedback is provided? Are the employees given a copy of their results, and assured that any other copies are confidentially and securely locked away?

A company's attitude to psychological testing reveals much about how progressive they are, how caring they are and how committed they are to the importance of their human resource assets. This insight can be very useful in helping a prospective employee in deciding whether or not to join a company, and those administering the tests should be aware of this.

Ideally, a company using psychological testing will, in the process, heighten its employees' perceptions of its care and approach to developing management excellence. When a company has to make a decision between candidates for a position, and when it is clear that they cannot all be successful, those who are turned away – or, preferably, come to an agreement that this specific opportunity is not for them at this particular time – should retain a favourable impression.

A well-chosen battery of psychological tests – with extensive feedback – combined with a thoughtfully conducted personal interview, will achieve this objective, with both successful and unsuccessful candidates. Selection procedures should be carefully designed to fit the job and the person being sought. And it should never be forgotten that the recruitment process is also all about marketing the company, in public relations terms. The most sensitive PR audience for any company is the group of people who were unsuccessful for jobs there: what will they say about the company in the market place? They will certainly have an opinion, and the employer should go to some lengths to ensure that it is an accurate one. Going for a job is very much a two-way process and the unsuccessful applicants will take away with them an impression of how they were handled that cannot be rectified later.

Companies with long traditions of using psychological testing enjoy the cumulative benefits of having built up a large databank of normative data, based on the past population, and can develop a picture of their 'employee most likely to succeed' against a given job specification. This encourages clarity and disciplined thinking about matching people with jobs. The careful use of well-chosen psychological tests has become, over the last three decades, the hallmark of a good employer.

THE ACCEPTABILITY OF PSYCHOLOGICAL TESTS

Some of the tests most favoured by many employers and candidates are not deemed scientifically valid or reliable by psychologists. Some tests are well received because of their strong face validity – or user friendliness – and are often very useful as a counselling tool, even though they are not seen as valid in a scientific sense.

It is important to remember the distinctions between scientific validity, scientific reliability and face validity. Tests which are scientifically valid and reliable can lack face validity and thus appear pointless. If no one wants to do the test because it seems to be a waste of time, then that test has failed the public relations test, however scientifically proven it may be.

The acceptability of psychological tests has been increased greatly by the advent of the computer, and the effect of this on the candidate/tester relationship. The tester is no longer the person who administers and scores the test; instead, he or she is the person who explains the point of it at the outset, and debriefs afterwards. The candidate is interacting with the machine, which then helps them to come to terms with the tester.

I believe that much to the traditional British fear of psychologists stemmed originally from the War Office procedure of sending all officer candidates for 'an interview with the psychologist'. This was interpreted by many to mean **PSYCHIATRIST**, and therefore 'shrink'. Even now, the distinction between the two is imperfectly understood. The fear of being mentally undressed by this individual was particularly heightened by the characteristic British sense of reserve, provoking a typical stiff-upper-lip reaction. The psychologist/psychiatrist was not seen as a human being just doing his or her job, but as a holder of secret weapons which would be used to lay bare the defenceless individual's inner soul.

The adoption of computers in psychological testing has helped to mitigate this legacy of fear and apprehension. The candidate uses the computer to gain self-knowledge, and then sees the psychologist afterwards, who will help with the interpretation. The psychologist's role is developmental, not judgemental. The computer has liberated the candidate to remain a person, and liberated the psychologist to be a counsellor.

MATCHING PEOPLE TO COMPANY CULTURES

It is important to bear in mind models of company cultures when assessing psychological tests and the types of personality they define. One of the principal purposes of using psychological testing effectively is to select people to work in certain cultures, or to understand *why* people are effective or not effective in their existing company or organisation. The model of company or organisation cultures outlined here has been used to appraise the value of certain psychological tests in the following test summaries, especially in terms of looking at the 'value of the test to the user organisation'.

There are many models of company cultures but the following simple model of four types from Ashridge Management College is useful. This classifies all companies into four types:

the **macho** culture;
the **process** culture;
the **retail** culture;
the **high-risk, slow-feedback** culture.

The **macho** culture attracts individualistic, high-risk operators who like a quick feedback of their results; people who will find a mountain and climb it. Many consultancies and advertising agencies have macho cultures, and this group would also include magazine companies and newspaper companies.

Process cultures include local authorities and capital goods manufacturers, companies in which technical expertise is very important. Process cultures are concerned with how the work is done and attention to detail, and often the customer and end-user are not particularly important. The method of working, however, is all important, and people in process cultures tend to focus on the actual process of their work.

In a **retail** culture, people work hard and play hard, and are very customer-driven. This culture favours vast action but low risk with frenetic activity selling high-demand products, such as hamburgers: for example McDonald's. There are strict, laid-down rules; decision-making is easy, and feedback is rapid.

This is in considerable contrast with a **high-risk, slow-feedback** culture such as the aircraft industry and design-oriented capital goods companies such as Rolls-Royce. It can take seven or eight years of research to create a new aero-engine, and even then someone else might make a better one. It can take a long time to find out if the decisions made at the time will turn out to have been the right ones.

It is essential to consider these cultures when matching people to job roles. Each psychological test considered here is examined in terms of its value in indicating the extent to which a person will or will not fit into a specific culture. See, under each test, the section entitled 'Value of the Test to the User Organisation'.

WHAT THIS BOOK DOES NOT COVER

It has only been possible to cover a short selection of the most popular psychological tests in this book. There are two forms of psychological testing in particular which have been omitted: these are **the DiSC system**, and **graphology**.

DiSC stands for the four specific personality traits it claims to identify: dominance, influence, submission and compliance. They are available as cheap software packages for personnel officers and managers to run themselves. Candidates who are put through such tests during interviews and in other situations are unlikely to understand much of what is going on. They will usually be presented with a form comprising four columns of apparently unrelated words, then asked to look at each row of words and choose the ones that fit their personality most and least accurately.

Using a complex system of scoring, the DiSC programme then produces a series of graphs, from which a personality report is derived. This gives insights into the characteristics of the person being tested, such as their attention to detail or lack of it, behaviour and reactions under stress, and ability to work unsupervised.

DiSC has come under attack recently from psychological researchers, who regard the theory which it depends on as flawed. However, DiSC is very popular, and well worth considering as a cheaper alternative to a number of the more expensive tests, especially when cost is an important consideration.

Graphology – understanding personality through handwriting analysis – is not a psychological test as such, but it is difficult to categorise it as anything else, and certainly it is playing an increasing part in selection and career development. The acceptance of graphology is on the increase, and the practice has many faithful adherents in mainland Europe. In France graphology gurus have attached themselves to a number of large employers, and their work is viewed with considerable credibility. Elsewhere it has not been accepted with such enthusiasm.

Glossary

Occupational psychology comes with its own special jargon. This section defines and describes the words highlighted in the introduction (such as **ABSTRACT**) and many others mentioned during the test summaries. This glossary is intended to offer a brief, basic explanation of words occurring in the book which may not be familiar to non-psychologists. More detailed definitions may be obtained by consulting the books listed under Further Reading at the end of the book.

For the person being tested, it will help you to become aware of the buzz words used in the world of occupational psychology. You don't want to be fazed by hearing these words and not knowing what they mean. For the inexperienced user, these definitions will certainly help you to pin-point the characteristics of different tests.

ABSTRACT
Used in the expression 'abstract reasoning', as opposed to verbal and numerical reasoning. 'Abstract', as a concept, is concerned with the representation of ideas in geometrical and other designs. A person being asked to undertake an abstract test is by definition being asked to establish relationships and recognise patterns between different, similar, or the same geometrical designs.

APPLICATIONS
As in 'applications of psychological tests', including selection, induction, team-building and career development, as well as crisis intervention. Most tests in this book are concerned with recruitment. Besides recruitment, applications are principally designed for improving performance and communication skills.

CLINICAL
Opposite of occupational psychology. Clinical psychology is concerned with observation, and strictly objective applications in the field of mental well-being. Clinical psychology looks at the resolution of internal conflicts.

COMPETENCE
This is concerned with fitness, efficiency, capacity and sufficiency. Measurable competencies are seen in middle-management terms as highly specific measurable features, whereas in senior management there is a greater concern with capacity more than competency. The concept of competency is thus much more nebulous at the senior level. Competence is specifically defined by occupational psychologists as utilising and facilitating the use of resources to maximum effect, in three areas: managing resources and systems; sensitivity to the environment and external factors; and personal effectiveness.

EXVIA
Cattell's word for Extraversion vs Introversion (see page 59 for Cattell). Such people are gregarious, sociable, competitive and enthusiastic. Its opposite is Invia.

FEEDBACK
This refers to an opportunity to discuss and explore the results of a person's assessment, considering this in terms of its implications for suitability for a particular job or promotion, and various aspects of personal and occupational development.

INDEX
This refers statistically to a comparison between a number of variables, but psychologically to an indicator of certain features within a personality, as in Sweney's Stress Index.

INDICATOR
This reference to features of a personality is less specific than 'test results'. 'Indication', by contrast, marks basic preferences and tendencies. For example, the Myers Briggs Type Indicator suggests certain character traits rather than concrete, black-and-white results or categories.

INSTRUMENT
This is simply another name for a test, in so far as it is a tool used to measure things.

INTERPRETATION
This refers to making sense of results in the context of psychological tests and understanding those test results in terms of the

necessary applications. Tests can be interpreted in a variety of ways according to the context.

INVENTORY
This implies a listing of features rather than an assessment or test. An inventory is more objective and less judgemental than a test.

IPSITIVE
This refers to a test which includes multiple choice questions, and that the sum of all the options expressed add up to a constant. The opposite of ipsitive is normative, which is looking for indications to compare against a specific norm group.

MODE
This describes the way of operating of a person, according to their way of reacting to a given situation. Some people operate in a variety of modes, others are more restricted in the varieties of the way they behave.

MOTIVATION
This is classified into three elements by occupational psychologists: need for achievement, need for affiliation, and need for power. The power motivation itself breaks down into four different elements (see Omega Motivation and Competency Inventory). More generally, the word motivation is used to describe aptitude and keenness.

NORMS
This relates to types and the ordering of the most frequent value or state. People should be compared against their norm group, i.e. people like themselves. The word normal comes from this word and implies the reflection of a standard against which one is compared. Breaking the norm is seen as being outside of one's usual group.

OCCUPATIONAL
This relates to one's job and one's working environment and, in the expression 'occupational psychology', is used in contrast to clinical psychology. Occupational psychology is concerned with studying people who are employed or occupied in a craft, trade or profession.

PATHEMIA

Pathemic people tend to feel rather than think. They are good-natured, attentive, trusting and warm-hearted. Pathemia and its opposite, Cortertia, are terms created by Cattell.

PERCENTILES

This means the value below which a specified percentage may fall. If all individuals are ranked in groups of the highest and lowest, according to raw scores, the percentile ranks of a particular individual is a percentage of the total group who are ranked below this individual. If we are told that a person's percentile rank on a test is 22, we know that person scored higher than 22 per cent of the people taking the test.

PERSONALITY

This summarises the nature of a person's existence in terms of the individual, distinctive and well-marked characteristics. Personality refers to an integration of all the psychological, intellectual, emotional and physical characteristics of an individual, especially according to how it is presented to other people.

POPULATION

This refers to the number of people in the norm group, i.e. the number of people which one is being compared against. Population refers to the people in a class considered statistically together.

PREDICTIVE

This means a test relating to the future behaviour of a person. Some tests are static, i.e. describing only present features, whereas predictive tests say something about how an individual will behave in a given situation, even if this has not been encountered before.

PROFILE

This means a summary or short biographical sketch, and is used generally by psychologists in bringing out the main characteristics of their tests, such as the DMT Profile or the Insight Profile, for example.

PSYCHOANALYSIS

This is the investigation of psychological forces making up a personality, as originally defined by Freud. This is the theory that the mind can be divided into conscious or subconscious elements.

PSYCHODYNAMIC
This pertains to mental and emotional forces, including those from past experience, and their effects on the present. The DMT is a psychodynamic test.

PSYCHOLOGY
Basically, this is the science of the mind. Psychological testing is a broader concept than psychometric testing, encompassing a number of varieties of psychological tests.

PSYCHOMETRIC
This is a branch of psychology dealing with measurable factors, which can be clearly and specifically added up, and the person given a score. This is not to be confused with psychometry, the measurement of the duration of mental processes and the faculty of divining an unknown person's qualities by handling objects used by them.

QUESTIONNAIRE
This refers to a type of test which includes a series of questions for comparison. A questionnaire result shows a variety of features rather than testing particular abilities.

RAW SCORE
This is the basic score before being converted into percentiles against the norm group.

RESPONSE
A person's reaction to a given situation or stimuli, a feature that all psychological tests are concerned with examining.

RESULTS
The scored, finalised features of a test as presented in the feedback session to the individual.

SCORING
The appraisal of test results according to the aim of the test, and according to the norm group.

STATIC
As opposed to predictive, static tests look at a person's behaviour

now rather than in the future. Sometimes they are indicative of future behaviour, sometimes not.

STEN SCORE
This is a way of scoring results according to an index, usually from 1 to 10, in specific psychometric tests which look at gradations and degrees of a certain type or behaviour.

TEST
This word is used generally in this book as synonymous with questionnaire, assessment, inventory or instrument, but specifically it means trial of fitness for examination. Scientifically it means a specific look for certain indicators.

TESTEE
Used in this book as the person being tested, known in psychologists' jargon as 'the subject'.

TESTER
Used in this book to refer to the person administering the test who may be a professional psychologist, but who also may be a person who holds a licence from the psychological testing company. Thus testers can be in-house or out-house.

TYPES
Another word for categories, used here to identify elements of personality and group them into certain defined groups.

USER
Used in this book to signify the employer who requests the tests to be carried out, the client of the psychological testing company and the person who buys the test.

VALIDITY
This relates to the effectiveness, adequacy and substantiated nature of a test. Face validity is an expression concerning the way the test appears to the testee. A test with high face validity looks to the testee like a useful, meaningful exercise with relevant questions. A test with low face validity can be rejected by suspicious and unconvinced testees.

Insights and Perspectives

The insights presented here are included to explain why certain tests have been chosen for coverage in this book, in terms of:

- Their usefulness and popularity among users.
- What the psychologists think of them.
- What it feels like (as a testee) to do the tests and receive feedback.
- How a professional views psychological tests.

Considerable research was carried out among all these categories of people with experience of psychological testing to decide upon the 19 tests selected here.

These perspectives are intended to introduce the particular tests chosen, and to raise a number of important issues, seen as concerns by users, testers, testees and specialists. These issues are not pursued in depth: it must be emphasised that this book is an introductory guide prepared for non-specialists by a non-specialist, and does not intend to go into the detail with which professional psychologists are concerned.

USERS' PERSPECTIVES

A user of psychological testing in a large financial services organisation

This user of psychological tests, who does not wish to be named, is constantly being approached by testing companies offering their services. He has extensive needs for testing, so their approaches are not without justification. But he finds it difficult to decide between the tests being offered, and needs to be convinced of their practical value before proceeding to use them on an extensive scale. He has found a number of them to be particularly suitable, and discusses them below:

OPQ
DMT
Myers Briggs
PAPI

'We have quite a few problems with some of our young traders and analysts. We invest a lot of time and effort in training them, only to find that either they leave us and go elsewhere, or that they are basically rather unstable, can't stand the pace and burn out.

'I have been particularly impressed by the value of the DMT in predicting which of our young traders will make it. This test was developed to identify potentially-successful fighter pilots for the Swedish Air Force, and I guess that there are relatively few differences between being a successful combat pilot and being a successful stockbroker. You must have cool nerves, good judgement, emotional stability and belief in yourself.

'We have substantially improved our track record in developing young brokers through the DMT. We still lose people to competitors, but at least now we are able to identify those who will or won't make it. Those who don't appear to have the drive, or lack emotional security, or who are contemptuous of authority and rock the boat too much in the office, we are able to weed out before appointment. We have also used the DMT on existing staff, and then deploy them as appropriate. Using the DMT widely throughout the organisation has proved expensive, but it has saved us from making some expensive mistakes.

'We also use more conventional psychological tests, such as OPQ, PAPI and Myers Briggs. These help us a great deal in team-building. We are part of a Japanese multinational, and Japanese management techniques tend to revolve around teams. We use psychological tests to determine which of the people we consider for appointment are most appropriate for the culture of this organisation. I have a masters' degree in psychology, so I am already converted to the idea, but it is still confusing to be faced with the variety of tests on the market place. It is a question of trial and error, and deciding which suits your needs best, and then sticking with it.'

John Smith of Succession Planning Associates (SPA), an executive search firm specialising in public sector appointments in the UK

This user has been working in the executive search business for more than 10 years, and in this time his attitude to psychological tests has changed dramatically. He uses a number of tried and tested instruments available on the market, but has developed his own proprietary test with the help of a psychologist. He discusses the tests he has used:

SPQR
GMA Systems
The Insight Profile
OPQ
Myers Briggs

'I find that many of the most popular personality tests are full of Americanisms, which tend to put off my candidates. For example, lots of them don't know what 'pep' is, or who 'sophomores' are. We have developed our own special instrument for our own purposes, the Succession Planning Questionnaire Response, SPQR. This was developed with a psychologist with whom we have worked for several years.

'It is important to us that our candidates are happy about doing our tests. For this reason, we don't give people too many tests or ones which are too long or tedious. I feel that long sessions of tests are counter-productive. Many more people are being tested nowadays, and will accept doing short tests, especially those with a high degree of face validity.

'We find that if candidates are asked to spend a whole day being tested, then they place too much weight on the results. It makes them anxious, because they think that the outcome of the entire selection process will depend upon it. It is logical for them to reason that if a whole day is spent on testing, and half a day on an interview, then the testing must be more important. Tests have become longer and longer as different testing companies try to sell more products, and more sophisticated products. Many of the users, both employers and executive search consultants, cannot judge which is necessarily the best test, and are often quite attracted to these very long and complex instruments. I used to favour them myself, but not any more.

'We spend a total of between two and a half and three hours on testing our candidates, on average. Typically, we would give people the Insight Profile test, which takes between 15 and 20 minutes to complete; OPQ 5, which takes between 30 and 40 minutes; SPQR, which takes from 10 to 15 minutes; and then we would carry out a series of ability tests, related to the job in question. We would use Saville & Holdsworth or GMA in numeracy, verbal and abstract reasoning. So we would spend about half of the testing time on personality tests.

'I recently heard of complaints by a number of candidates being put through tests of between three and six hours, and there have been instances when an entire field of candidates have walked out and refused to undertake the tests they have been asked to do. Inevitably, there will be other instances of this, and this will put pressure on users to have shorter tests for selection purposes.

'Career development is another issue, of course, and for these some of the longer tests are highly relevant. The key difference is the fact that selection tests are carried out in the candidate's time, and career development tests are carried out in the company's time. People don't mind tests for selection purposes if they can be seen to have a value. I used to be keen on longer tests, but I have certainly changed my mind, and tried to resist the efforts of testing companies to sell me more and more tests.

'I am very concerned that many employers place too much emphasis on the results of tests, which effectively lets them off the hook in making selection decisions. When the candidates are aware of this, it can make them quite neurotic about how to answer the tests.

'What is the employer looking for? It is particularly worrying for people who have never done a test before. I always ask candidates I am testing if they have done personality tests before. If they haven't, I will give them the opportunity to do a fairly standard test, such as OPQ 3, as a dummy run. This helps them to be familiar with the test process and takes away the disadvantage which they may face in competition with other candidates. If someone has never done a test before, to be suddenly confronted by about three hours of tests can be quite daunting and can affect their performance. We try to give all our candidates a level playing field, as it were.

'So, to sum up, we use our own test, SPQR, together with Insight, OPQ 5, and we sometimes use other tests. For large numbers of non-executive candidates, we would consider using Thomas International, but this is not so useful for senior people. We also use Myers Briggs, and we look at a person's Belbin team type which we can get from the OPQ. We use personality tests for practically every appointment we handle in local government. We see that test results are useful, as they are one more set of information and we use them at the sifting stage, before the candidate goes to the client. Many of our candidates will do half a day at the client's later, so we don't overdo it with tests that are too long and involved at this stage. In this initial sift, OPQ and Insight are used as key tools, and we use SPQR mostly for leadership assessment.

'Why are we so keen about personality tests? We argue that when senior people fail to make a success of a senior appointment, it is nearly always due to a clash of personality. We make our own appraisal of the personality of the client and the needs of the job, so we can make an appraisal of the personality of candidates which complement them. I find that it is vital, first of all, to fit the ethos of people to the ethos of the organisation, and therefore I always like to do personality testing before presenting a candidate to a client.

'Although many of the clients subsequently test people, I insist on my own tests, and I see this as part of the SPA deal. In the public sector, it is easier to be quite open in the process of selection. We have to be totally confident that they can do the job, but also we must be sure that their personality will fit the organisation. So even when clients don't want to use testing, we always insist upon it. We play quite a dynamic part in the testing process.

'Some of our clients are concerned that our tests are culturally biased, but we don't believe this. We maintain that they are entirely bias free. Some of our clients think that we are doing things in a black box in a rather mysterious way, but we explain to them exactly what is happening, as we do to our candidates.

'However, we don't give feedback to the candidates until after the appointment has been made. We feel that if they know their test results and they're still within the selection process, they may modify their behaviour to offset some of the results of the tests. Doing this may not be in their best interests. We want our candidates just to be themselves and not try to be something different. If they got the job on the basis of modifying their behaviour as a result of a test, clearly they would have to carry on permanently modifying their behaviour, which might be a strain. It would be completely dishonest to try to get a job on the basis of a false representation of your personality, and you would then have to sustain it, and end up living a lie.

'In over four years, only one candidate has withdrawn from a test, but some people may decide not to put themselves forward in the first place because they don't like the idea of doing tests. It's very important how candidates are treated and they must realise that a test is reasonable and worth doing. They should not think the whole basis of the selection decision will be the test.'

Yvonne Sarch of Sarch Search International, an international executive search firm

This user has considerable experience of psychological assessment in selection, and hires various psychologists to help with her recruitment needs on behalf of her clients. She is particularly interested in combinations of tests for certain uses. She points to certain problems experienced in her use of testing services, particularly those psychologists who try to do her job for her. She discusses a number of tests below:

OPQ
Myers Briggs
16-PF
PAPI
Belbin
Omega Motivation and Competency Inventory
graphology

'I use psychological testing extensively on behalf of my clients in my executive search practice. I find that OPQ is a good off-the-shelf test, but with the important proviso that it's only as good as the psychologist who is administering it and providing the feedback. This can vary enormously, and it's hard to know whom to trust.

'I have found that, sometimes, psychologists are not content just to test the person and produce the results. Instead, they want to know all about the job the candidates are up for, and they want to make their own comments as to who is suitable. But this is my job, and they're not qualified in appraising and selecting people, and presenting them to the client. They try to put their own perspectives on the person, and try and match them against a specific job.

'Quite frankly, I don't need this; I just want a professional psychologist who will handle the testing exercise for me. The whole thing hangs on how good a psychologist is at explaining a subjective interpretation. We don't want psychologists trying to be headhunters too!

'I always favour tests of people working in groups, because it is inappropriate only to test people as individuals. In these scenarios, including a psychologist and observers, it is possible to see which of the individuals participating will take the lead, which is the hunter, which is the trouble-maker, and which of the people talk first and think second, and vice versa. People definitely behave differently in groups. The Belbin Team Roles exercise is certainly more relevant than many other tests in this regard.

'The 16-PF, Myers Briggs and OPQ have emerged as favourites for general testing purposes, but one hiccup is now emerging: it has now got to the point where too many people have done them before. So there is a constant need to produce new versions, which clearly keeps the psychologists in business. The corollary of this is that the person who has not done such tests before can be at a big disadvantage, and should find out about the various tests available, and gain opportunities to practice.

'The Belbin role model is good, and this sets people off thinking about themselves and their colleagues, in group situations. Too many tests are simply geared toward testing individuals in isolation. The Motivation and Competency Inventory by Omega is also useful, but it has become very complex. This test is now so sophisticated that it can be difficult to understand from the point of view of the user or person being tested. A test which is only comprehensible to another psychologist is not of much use.

'The PAPI test is very popular with people who have done it, and received the feedback. They like it, and want to use it as a tool in the selection process. Both PAPI and OPQ are good within batteries of tests. They provide a good foundation from which to look at testing other qualities and attributes. Few tests are good enough to be used on their own and, of course, no test or tests can take the place of good structured interviews by a real professional.'

TESTERS' PERSPECTIVES

Whitehead Mann Audit & Assessment

This organisation is the subsidiary of a leading British executive search firm, Whitehead Mann, itself part of a larger, international search operation, named Amrop. The assessment service was initially founded to serve existing clients of the parent company, but it has now built up its own portfolio of clients. It does not produce its own proprietary tests, but has put together a number of innovative packages of tests. Rob Irving, the director, discusses a number of tests and what he sees as the most important issues in psychological testing:

DMT
OPQ
FIRO-B
GMA Abstract
Sweney's Decision Profile
Sweney's Stress Index
Fleishman's Leadership Opinion Questionnaire
Thomas-Kilman Modes of Conflict Instrument
The Bortner Type A Questionnaire

'There are important ethical questions about assessment techniques. When a company takes someone on, they clearly want to know about him or her, and need to be aware of the particular managerial skills and qualities of each individual on the payroll. Thus, they need to be able to use a range of tests to reveal these skills and qualities in an accurate and meaningful way.

'However, we believe that it is not necessarily ethical for a company to subject employees to clinical-type tests which analyse their past emotional experiences and their emotional development from their childhood to the present. Most occupational tests have been developed to explore surface traits, and basic personality types can be revealed without the use of clinical tests. There could be a debate here that more clinical tests, such as the DMT (although widely used in an occupational setting), have little relevance in a job situation. Others may disagree, but we would not want to use this type of test ourselves. We specialise in shorter tests geared very much for the occupational setting, and choose combinations of tests designed specifically for our clients.

'We favour the basic psychometric tests, which are quick to do and quick to score, and which have a published validity. These are quite distinct from the clinical tests, which are conceptually totally different. These quick instruments are, arguably, more important and relevant in the job setting than the longer, more complex assessment. For example, the short Bortner Type A Questionnaire can offer some very useful, quick insights, laying the foundations for further tests.

'We select from tests available, and use a blend of different instruments, put together as a test battery. Most of these tests have been validated in a Whitehead Mann setting, on our own clients. The aim is to make an objective assessment of surface traits rather than an in-depth clinical analysis.

'In terms of the popular OPQ test, we have developed our own norms, representing a more senior managerial and professional group than the standard Saville & Holdsworth norm. There are significant differences in the results of a test normed against Saville & Holdsworth's graduate and middle-management test, compared with the Whitehead Mann norms [these are discussed under the OPQ summary]. The OPQ is a very successful test, but those being tested need to be normed against the most relevant group for maximum accuracy and benefit.

'We have discovered and utilised a range of American instruments which enable the company to offer useful batteries of occupational-related tests. These include Sweney's Decision Profile and Stress Index, the Thomas-Kilman Modes of Conflict Instrument, and Fleishman's Leadership Opinion Questionnaire.

'We have found these tests to be relevant, revealing and highly appropriate to the needs of our clients. We are quite surprised that few other assessment organisations in the UK offer them. None of these tests takes very long to do, but each looks at people from a different perspective. Together, they can provide a very detailed insight into the psychological profile of an individual at work. Singly they may appear limited and slightly esoteric, but together they are powerful and convincing.

'We are not wedded to one set of instruments, but we make a selection according to the needs of the client. We are critical of testing which offers inadequate follow up.

'In the USA, there is considerable legislation and regulation of test usage, but in the UK, testing activities are generally under-regulated, and, arguably, there could be some restriction of this activity.

'Psychological tests are fundamentally discriminatory, if only in terms of the effect upon people who have not done tests before. The Post Office did a study on test practice and the effect on test results of experience in having done tests generally. People who are familiar with tests tend to take them in their stride much more easily than those who have not done them before.

'We also arrange ability tests, including the GMA test battery of ability and abstract reasoning tests. The GMA includes verbal, numeric and abstract tests. These are among the most popular tests for these purposes. The abstract test is especially relevant for senior executives who need to have an ability in strategic thinking.

'We believe that tests should not be used to make judgements on people as being employable or not employable. Instead, we argue that people are assets, and we need to understand the best way to use them both as a leader and as a subordinate, and also as a member of a team. Our added value comes from our choice of tests to suggest for particular applications, detailed feedback to each person being tested, and relevance of the test to the person, in helping them to the best advantage in a particular environment.'

Omega Management Consultants

This company has long-established expertise in occupational psychology, and has perfected its own special battery of tests, known as the Motivation and Competence Inventory, offered in a variety of forms. Dr George New of Omega is critical of so-called superficial tests, and feels that there is an extensive degree of misrepresentation and misuse of these tests. He discusses his own test and others below, together with his main concerns:

Motivation and Competence Inventory
Myers Briggs

'Myers Briggs is extensively used for selection purposes in the UK, when it was never designed for this particular purpose. This is true of many other tests. Unfortunately, many tests are used in the UK as a substitute for interviewers' judgement, rather than as an adjunct, to help remove responsibility from the personnel people who are trying to avoid it.

'Yet, there are many elements in selection and career development which cannot be satisfactorily tested, such as 'Do you like your job?', 'Will you like a move to another job?', 'Is your job socially acceptable to you?' Many personnel people accused of poor recruiting will blame the tests which are traditionally used in their departments, when they are, in fact, using the tests in an entirely wrong way. The more superficial tests give personnel managers a false sense of security, and there will be a backlash against their use in the near future.

'It is important to talk to users of tests, to look at the numbers of companies and recruiters who use testing as an important step in recruiting. Which people interviewed well but were rejected on their test results? Are people offered jobs on the basis of their test results being acceptable, even if their interview was less successful? Does everyone get individual and confidential feedback after each test? Or, do they just get a rejection letter from the potential employer? Are there cases of people spending a whole day completing a variety of psychological tests who then hear nothing more about them? Everyone should receive feedback so that they can have the benefit of having done the test, even if they don't get the job or the promotion.

'We have developed our Motivation and Competence Instrument over several years to present a rounded view of each individual, to go below the surface. Too many tests can be easily falsified. You could give me a number of popular, superficial tests and I could give you results to order to show anything you like. This is not possible with our test. We take a sample of the mind of each individual. It is impossible to show yourself to be anything other than you are.'

Pintab Associates

This company has been offering what it calls 'psychodynamic assessment' over the last decade, including a range of instruments not commonly used by competitors. They have built up a niche position serving the needs of clients looking for sophisticated tools for selection and, especially, career development. Olya Khaleelee, a Pintab consultant, discusses their tests and the issues:

DMT
The Colour Test
Watson Glaser Critical Thinking Analysis
Raven's Progressive Matrices

'We have developed a number of batteries of tests and assessment combinations, and in the course of the years we have found these four forms of assessment to be particularly valuable.

'Watson's and Raven's are used quite widely as ability tests, but we tend to use them to test abstract thinking in senior executives. They are particularly valuable in selecting people for top jobs. They are used in both job selection, and in career development and succession planning.

'We have found the DMT to be particularly revealing. The results of different candidates for one job can be startlingly different. The DMT provides real insight into psychological makeup, and can reveal deep-seated traits which would be missed by the standard occupational tests. Personally, I never cease to be amazed by what it shows. But it is not for the mass market. We gear this for senior executives only.

'Similarly, the Colour Test is used to analyse inner recesses of thinking, especially in terms of high-level managerial capacity. It requires a very professional approach to feedback and interpretation.

'These tests deserve to be taken very seriously indeed. They have been developed over a long period of time and have considerable norm groups. They are uniquely appropriate in certain settings, but are not for everyone. We serve a closely-defined niche market.'

TESTEES' PERSPECTIVES

A variety of testees, most of whom had taken a range of tests over the years, were asked to talk about each of the ones included in this book. Some opinions were positive, some negative, but all bring up interesting points. When you do the test yourself you may agree with this sample or you may feel differently.

PAPI

'I thought that this was quite a fun test to do, though it was difficult to choose between the statements. I often thought that both of them were irrelevant and inappropriate, and it annoyed me to say that one thing was true of me when I thought it wasn't, although it was more acceptable than the other alternative. I like the wheel design used in the feedback, and the easy-to-understand summary of the findings. It did match my personality and tendencies at work quite accurately, although some were rather exaggerated. Altogether, it was well worth doing, but it did tend to whet my appetite for more rather than answer all the questions I had in mind. It scratched the surface rather than deeply penetrating it.'

Myers Briggs Type Indicator

'This is one of my all-time favourites. The personality types are very well thought-out and are good summaries of basic outlook. Yet I have heard that this test can be used to make sure that everyone in a certain organisation is of the same type, and I don't think I would agree with this. The test itself has quite an American style, but is fairly international in application. The test seems to be pretty accurate, because I made a guess of the type I thought I was before doing the test, and came out as I and the psychologist expected.'

16-PF

'I didn't think that this was quite as straightforward as the Myers Briggs. Some of the questions seemed rather inappropriate. It seemed a bit old-fashioned, and I wasn't that convinced about the feedback. It seemed a bit extreme in the results, and I was warned that it tended to show up bi-polar findings. Some of it seemed a bit childish, and the statements rather glib. I think I would have preferred to choose between just two statements, rather than have an in-between option too. But I can imagine that many would find it useful.'

OPQ 4.2

'I did this test by computer, which had a certain amount of novelty value, and it was not boring. It was very efficiently administered. There is an advantage doing it this way: you don't feel you're being tested by a person, but by a machine, and it seems more detached. But for me the results-by-machine was less of a good idea. The analysis booklet seemed rather cold and formal, and did not reflect the findings as well as I'm sure a good psychologist could. OK, it is quick to score this way, and 10 minutes after finishing the test I was presented with an impressive booklet. The OPQ does give you a huge amount of insight about yourself, it's just a question of how you interpret it.'

FIRO-B

'This test did not seem so geared towards the work setting as many others. The questions seemed to be mostly about your relation-ships with people, more at home and socially than at work, although I can see that it does have occupational uses. It was relatively easy to do, and quite good in showing how independent and/or sociable you are. It certainly showed another dimension to my personality compared with other tests. I would have thought that it wouldn't be a huge amount of use on its own, but best combined with other, more job-oriented assessments.'

GMA Abstract Test

'I found this extremely difficult to do. These were real brain-teasers. They started off easy, and then became very difficult indeed. Someone with a real talent for abstract reasoning would enjoy this, but not me. The aim is to see relationships between unconnected things, and plan for the long term. They come out well in this test. It's very much an ability test, but throws interest-ing light on personality too.'

Sweney's Decision Profile

'This is an excellent short test on how you make your decisions. The questions are straightforward and highly appropriate to how you go about making decisions, and the sort of decisions you make. It depends rather on the honesty of the person doing the test, but if you do it as honestly and frankly as possible, it offers a very good summary of your attitude to decision-making. It is rather limited in scope, but very good for what it is. It could do with being translated from American into English, but is very good generally.'

Sweney's Stress Index

'There is clearly an important reason for including this test in any battery. If you answer the questions as truthfully as possible, it does show up where you are suffering from stress. Thankfully I wasn't too stressed generally, but there were a few places of concern, which the psychologist explained. I'm going to try to do something about these. I liked the way that this test was so closely focused. It was well worth doing. It should be included in all general batteries.'

Fleishman's Leadership Opinion Questionnaire

'This is a very well thought-out test, and one of the few to examine this question of leadership in such a thoughtful way. It doesn't say that certain types of leadership are good or bad, but just identifies your own leadership style. The questions and the results were straightforward. It made you think about whether or not your style of leadership was appropriate. It was very American in style, reflecting the American rather than the British approach to leadership – which is very different – but it was still useful.'

Thomas-Kilman Modes of Conflict Instrument

'This was particularly fascinating and excellent in terms of how you deal with conflict. I had never thought that there were so many different ways of dealing with situations of conflict. It was certainly helpful in terms of the way I saw my role in teams. It would be very useful in selecting people for negotiating assignments. How you deal with conflict is a very important part of your daily life at work. Some companies encourage conflict much more than others.'

The Insight Profile

'This test is preceded by a lot of explanation about where it comes from. This is only necessary if you are really interested in psychology. It claims to simplify some of the complexities of many tests, and is good for showing where your basic drives come from. The feedback chart is very clear, although tends to show extremes. Not amazingly new and original, although useful in so far as it goes.'

SPQR

'A short, quite easy test which helpfully summarises management style. It has been developed in English, and is especially good at looking at how you work and where you are most effective. It has been refined and improved on the way, and this is clear when you do it. Useful for specific job areas, and without jargon.'

Omega Motivation and Competency Inventory

'This was the most amazingly long, detailed test. I felt I was being put through the wringer. I spent hours and hours answering multiple-choice questions, writing stories connected to pictures and composing a very detailed business plan. It was difficult to see how the results tied up to the work I had done. It was clearly expensive in time and money. It would be most useful when all the senior people in an organisation have completed it, and their jobs can be scoped out accordingly. I wouldn't have minded doing it if my employer was paying, but it was tough to give up a whole day to do it as part of a job interview.'

Raven's Progressive Matrices

'These were difficult puzzles, designed to see how well you could spot relationships and make logical deductions. It was a bit like going back to school, and reminded me of abstract exams I did as a child. The real value of these was explained in the feedback. They showed ability at conceptual thinking, and confidence in making judgements.'

Watson Glaser Critical Thinking Analysis

'These tests really made you think. They really stretched the mind. There was a lot to read, and a lot to take in and reason out before you could decide on the answers. It certainly separated the sheep from the goats. I can see why this test is used for high-level selection. It is excellent in terms of looking at how, and how well, you think things out. But would you be able to do it more than once?'

The Colour Test

'This was fun to do, but it wasn't clear to me if there was a connection with the business world. It was useful in looking at certain personality types, but not in terms of job applications. It would need to be combined with other tests. But it was intriguing to see what the choice of certain colours meant.'

The DMT

'This test changed the whole way I think about myself. I had no idea that my childhood had such an important impact on my current way of thinking. I had never thought about what drives me before, and where my attitudes to work and authority come from. Doing the test is quite mind-blowing. It's a very strange experience. I found myself talking about it for weeks afterwards. It certainly helps you to discover the makeup of your personality. It was almost uncanny in terms of accuracy and insights. I would defy anybody not to be moved by this. But having said all this, the DMT is not necessarily clearly related to your job, unless this is clearly explained in the feedback.'

Belbin's Team Role Model

'This was the most fun, and most difficult, of all the tests I've ever done, or ever heard of anyone doing. It was also the longest, involving having a couple of days off work, and not everyone could spare this. But it was really amazing to enact this special game to analyse how different team types behave. I certainly learned a lot about how some teams work well, and why others are chaotic or never produce results. However, I can't see how a company could implement the findings. They couldn't break up all the existing teams and regroup them on the basis of the Belbin types, as certain teams do certain things and need certain people in them regardless of their team type. Yet it does help you to be more tolerant of the weaknesses of those you work with.'

The Bortner Type A Questionnaire

'This is a very simple little test. It takes just a few minutes to do. It's useful in showing your broad personality type, which indicates how you will be subject to stress. Type A personalities certainly feel more stress than type Bs, and I found it useful to understand why.'

A PROFESSIONAL'S PERSPECTIVE

Barry Curnow, Principal of Maresfield Curnow and Immediate Past President of the Institute of Personnel Management

Barry Curnow has experienced the world of psychological testing in its different manifestations throughout his professional career, as a postgraduate student of Occupational Psychology, as an employer, in guiding clients on test usage, in counselling candidates on their test results and also in going through some form of systematic selection procedure himself for each successive appointment in his own career as a management consultant. The use of psychological testing continues to be an area of key concern in his current work training and developing management consultants at Maresfield Curnow and in providing coaching and mentoring to management consultants and their senior executive clients.

'All the tests mentioned in this book have their applications and value, but no test should ever be used in isolation when making a selection or career progression decision. They are tools to aid human resource decision-making, not a substitute for experienced judgement.

'Ideally, tests should provide insight into how the candidate might perform and respond to different situations for the purposes of job-matching, counselling and career planning. All tests should be prefaced with the necessary preliminary and explanatory information, and administered in neutral, non-threatening surroundings. The purpose and context of the test should be clearly understood from the outset.

'Psychological tests are a useful adjunct to the vital management job of assessment and selection, which is primarily an information-gathering function. This information should be derived from a variety of sources to build up a comprehensive picture of the individual. Psychological tests are one source, while others include bio-data and personal interviews. A systematic approach to human resource selection and development requires multiple inputs, of which psychological testing is one.

'Feedback is essential. Administering a test without offering feedback to the candidate is just as incomplete as a test without interpretation of results for the user would be, and is bad professional practice.

'Using psychological tests without contextual explanation or interactive feedback at best creates bad public relations for the company; at worst, it may even impose lasting damage on an individual, especially if the individual believes – usually incorrectly – that he or she is being denied a job appointment or career progression as a result of 'failing' a test.

'I feel that companies administering tests without appropriate preliminaries and follow-up should lose their licences or have them endorsed until they demonstrate good practice. Best practice is that candidates should have access to, or vetting rights over, test results, rather in keeping with the sort of safeguards available under the data protection provisions.

'The world of psychological testing has been fraught with controversy from its earliest days. One debate is concerned with the use of traditional, well-validated tests, over newer forms of testing. Many professional psychologists criticise the newer tests as being unreliable, invalid or both, and almost certainly gimmicky. However, many of the newer tests appeal widely to both users and candidates. They can appear modern and relevant, more appropriate to the working environment of the 1990s.

'A further debate – among users rather than psychologists – concerns the face validity, or user-friendliness, of tests generally.

There can be an irritability factor with some tests, in which it is hard to see what quality or perception is being tested, and why.

'Academic psychologists may criticise their applied psychologist colleagues for drifting away from the purity of controlled research and getting their hands dirty in the commercial market place, but I am a firm believer in the value of applied occupational psychology, and the traditions of "fitting the job to the person, and the person to the job".'

THE
TESTS

The PA Preference Inventory

Background

The PA Preference Inventory or PAPI, is now a highly popular workstyle questionnaire or assessment tool, and is growing in range of usage.

PAPI has become one of the key elements of the range of assessment services offered by the PA Consulting Group, a diversified, international consultancy organisation, involved in executive search, selection, executive leasing, outplacement and other human resources services. PAPI is used by PA for their clients and is licensed out to other organisations by PA.

PAPI, devised to form a basis for interview discussions, was designed by Dr Kostick, working in the State College of Boston, Massachusetts, in the 1960s, and it was first used by PA in 1966. PA gained the exclusive worldwide rights to market this questionnaire in 1979, and now many employers use it under licence from PA. PA runs training courses to instruct licence-holders in the most effective use of PAPI.

The aims of the test

PAPI is most useful as a mechanism for structuring an occupational discussion, whether for selection purposes, as part of a team-building exercise, or for a career planning, development and/ or counselling session. It does not seek to analyse personality in depth, and is not able to answer every question about an individual, but it is useful for opening up discussions around preferred workstyle.

PAPI has been devised to reveal the nature of people's preferred ways of working, and thus how they can most usefully be accommodated in an organisation. Following a discussion PAPI reveals for example an individual's preferred management style, indicates how an employee is likely to react in a given work or team situation, and also covers a range of other areas.

The format

PAPI is short, simple and fairly user-friendly, in that the person completing the questionnaire identifies preferences in 90 pairs of statements. The PA psychologists themselves describe PAPI as 'basic and helpful, truly work-related and extremely useful and versatile'. There are no rights and wrongs; it is merely a question of choosing between two phrases, in a fairly instinctive way rather than after long deliberation.

Range of applications

PAPI is typically used for supervisory roles and at all levels of management, in both recruitment situations and for existing employees. It can be carried out again later to assess changing work patterns and preferences over time.

Doing the test

The person completing the questionnaire is told that there are 90 pairs of statements, and that they must choose the statement in each pair which most closely describes them at work. There will be pairs of statements where it is difficult to make a choice, but the individual must nevertheless choose one. Each pair of statements should be judged independently, without bearing in mind how previous statements have been judged.

The layout of the PAPI document has been cleverly devised to expedite scoring, and only a small number of the total 90 questions can be seen at any one time, which stops the questionnaire from appearing daunting. The individual simply ticks the box next to the most appropriate – or least inappropriate – statement of each pair.

PAPI can be frustrating and puzzling because of the repetition of a number of phrases – exactly or similarly – and the fact that many individuals find it very hard to choose between them. That they are forced to choose is significant, and the effect of making these choices over 90 statements produces the end picture.

It is important for the testee to answer the questionnaire

honestly, and not to be guided by feedback already received from other tests they have done. The effect of the repetition of key concepts inhibits 'faking good'.

Inevitably, there are some ambiguities within PAPI, but relatively few. Some of the concepts and words used are rather American ('I usually have pep or vigor' and 'I am very cordial to people'), but PAPI is mostly international in style.

PAPI is not designed to be intellectually stretching, although it does tax one's decision-making powers. There is always some concern that the individual's feelings are not being accurately represented, given the unsatisfactory nature of some of the necessary choices. However, when PAPI is interpreted, the individual should be satisfied that their preferences are pinpointed with a large degree of insight, and the discussion will always allow context and subtleties to be highlighted.

Examples of content of the test

Choose one of the pair in each case: 'I am a hard worker' or 'I am not moody'; 'I usually work in a hurry' or 'I am always pleasant'; 'I make decisions easily and rapidly' or 'I keep my things neat and orderly', 'I like to follow rules carefully' or 'I like people to know me very well'.

There is some repetition of the statements, in different combinations, with emphasis on different words.

Time needed to complete the test

Can take as long as 20 minutes, or as little as 10 minutes. Either way, this is one of the shortest questionnaires of its kind available. Longer times may reflect a nervousness that the 'right' statements are being chosen, but individuals are encouraged to respond quickly to the statements without becoming too analytical about the exercise.

Time to score the test

PAPI is extremely quick to score, but may require a certain amount of time for considering interpretation before feedback discussion begins. This may follow immediately afterwards, or at a later date, but too long a gap is not considered advisable.

Necessary time for feedback

Feedback is an integral part of PAPI and is essential in all cases. It can be as short as half an hour, but this only allows time to scratch the surface of the findings. It is entirely possible to continue for an hour or more, whilst points are clarified and discussion deepens. The feedback of PAPI is a two-way process and 'ownership' of the results is key.

Format/structure of the feedback

PAPI is quick and easy, both to complete and to score, and to understand in discussion. The diagrammatic scoring sheet – summarised in a wheel-type design – provides a useful focus for the discussion. Thus, it comes with its own built-in feedback structure, looking at its 20 different factors, 7 key areas, 10 needs and 10 roles.

The 20 different factors fit into the 7 key areas in the following way.

Work direction	{ need to finish a task role of hard worker need to achieve
Leadership	{ leadership role need to control others ease in decision-making
Activity	{ work pace physical pace
Social nature	{ need to relate closely to individuals need to belong to groups social extension need for recognition
Workstyle	{ organised type interest in working with details reflective type
Temperament	{ need for change emotional control need to be forceful

Followership $\left\{\begin{array}{l}\text{need to be supportive} \\ \text{need for rules and supervision}\end{array}\right.$

Value to the employer/user

PAPI has become one of the most popular of the quick-to-administer instruments on the market, used by hundreds of employers and completed by thousands of employees/job candidates over the last 25+ years. PAPI is extensively used as a selection and development tool, but can be useful in a variety of other settings too. It gets the ball rolling in starting off a dialogue, and helps people to open up in interview situations.

Value to the employee/person being tested

PAPI is a good introduction to the world of psychological assessments: from the point of view of the person being assessed, it combines a somewhat perplexing format while the inventory is being completed, with a straightforward, insightful and highly rational end result. It also provides the individual with an opportunity to discuss their preferences at work, and to enter into the assessment process themselves.

Value to the user organisation

PAPI can be used to help fit people into organisational structures and styles, according to their work direction, temperament, workstyle and social nature. An individual's preferred style of working can be determined and consideration then given to how they will fit into the organisation with implications for training.

Can the test results be deliberately falsified?

With difficulty, because the questions do not seem to be directly related to work in organisations, and the element of forced choice which makes people decide on their responses is helpful in this.

Advantages over other tests

Quicker and easier than many, with simple and attractive feedback chart that is clear and understandable to those unfamiliar with psychological tests generally.

Disadvantages compared with other tests

Rather American in style, degree of repetition can be frustrating, perhaps rather simplistic to purists.

Tests may be combined with . . .

Can be used alone or can be combined with other instruments to provide a fuller assessment, such as Myers Briggs and 16-PF, which may give data on the underlying personality, thus adding to the view of the individual's preferred workstyle, as indicated by PAPI.

Static/predictive value

Clear view of the way a person currently operates, useful for structuring an interview to gather data to predict how he or she will behave in an occupational setting.

Overall review

Speed of being tested – fast
Speed of scoring results – fast
Cost – low
Range of applications – wide
In-house/Out-house – In-house under licence or Out-house at PA
Basic/Advanced – basic

How to prepare yourself for sitting this test

You must choose between pairs of statements throughout the questionnaire, even if this seems difficult. The statements are simple, straightforward and unambiguous. You should keep an open mind, even if some of the statements appear baffling.

It can be best to answer the points fairly quickly and efficiently, without spending too much time on each. Often the first instinct is the most telling. It can take longer if there is any confusion over what a certain statement means.

Will this test produce a different result after a period of time?

May do, as it reflects changing needs and working experiences. It would need to be repeated after a year to two years.

Myers Briggs Type Indicator

Background

Myers Briggs is an increasingly popular personality questionnaire which looks at thinking and relating styles, and offers a classification of 16 personality types. These are based on four different personality constructs, on the basis of Jungian psychology, which were identified and developed by three generations of the Briggs family, most recently by Isabel Briggs Myers. They have proceeded to build on Jung's theories and to apply these to an occupational setting, apparently very successfully.

This famous instrument, which first came out in about 1946, has now been extremely well validated, with extensive norm groups, and has become a favourite among a wide range of employers. The current version, now in widespread use both in the USA and the UK, was developed and copyrighted in 1976–7. It is distributed by Consulting Psychologists Press of California, and is now available through Oxford Psychologists Press in the UK.

The aims of the test

The Myers Briggs Type Indicator aims to classify people accurately according to specific personality types, which are now well respected and widely referred to in a variety of organisations. There are four bi-polar scales, producing 16 possible combinations or broad personality types. The categories are extroverts and introverts, sensing types and intuitive types, thinking types and feeling types, and judging and perceiving types.

The format

The Myers Briggs instrument includes 126 questions divided into three main parts. Each part is, in effect, a different way of looking at the same series of topics. The style of the questionnaire is not too American in terms of vocabulary, and is quite standard in format with clearly defined options.

Again, there are no right or wrong answers, and the person doing the questionnaire is asked to opt for preference a) or b) in each of the 126 questions, or in some cases, the c) option.

Range of Applications

Myers Briggs is used in career development, team-building, management development and sometimes in selection. It has a wide range of applications as a basic personality questionnaire, and is particularly appropriate at the beginning of a battery of different tests, especially because it is so user-friendly, and even pleasant and enjoyable to complete, certainly more than many of the other assessments.

Doing the test

In completing the Myers Briggs questionnaire, it is simply a case of answering a series of pairs of statements by choosing either a) or b). Occasionally, there is a third option c) too, and in one instance it is possible to choose two out of three options. The options are not too extreme, and in most cases it is easy to make a choice. Myers Briggs has been adapted considerably over time and has now been extensively refined to give it increased face validity. Of particular appeal is a section listing words, usually a series of opposites, but these are quite subtle (such as 'foundation' and 'spire', for example).

Examples of content of the test

(Not possible for copyright reasons.)

Time needed to complete the test

The Myers Briggs test takes about 20–30 minutes to complete.

Time to score the test

Can be quickly scored for the feedback session at the same meeting.

Necessary time for feedback

Can take around 30 minutes, but this depends on the objectives and can often be longer.

Format/structure of the feedback

The answers given in the score diagram reflect four separate preferences: either extrovert (E) or introvert (I); sensing (S) or intuitive (I); thinking (T) or feeling (F); and judging (J) or perceiving (P). Understanding the differences between these types is fundamental to making the most of this test. Each combination of preferences tends to be characterised by its own set of interests, values and skills.

In the feedback session, the person administering the assessment will analyse the subject's scores according to their preference for extroversion/introversion, sensing/intuitive, thinking/feeling, and judging/perceptive. Everyone doing this test will have specific preference scores according to their results, and these form the personality type, made up of a combination of four from the letters E, I, S, N, T, F, J, P. What do each of these preferences mean?

Being described as an **extrovert** means that you probably relate more easily to the outer world of people and things than to the inner world of ideas. An **introvert,** on the other hand, is more aware of what is going on inside their own mind. Much of this form of analysis is based on Jung's division of people into groups who like action and activity, and those who like their own space.

Much of it is a question of where you get your energy and drive from, and what takes away your energy and makes you feel drained. In extreme cases, it is sometimes hard for an extrovert to understand an introvert's form of activity and attitudes, and vice versa.

Then there is the second, bi-polar dimension, that of **sensing** compared with **intuition.** People who are sensing prefer to work with known facts rather than look for possibilities and relationships. Those with a high preference for intuition would rather look for possibilities and relationships than work with known facts. Sensing people are practical, cautious and handle routine well. By contrast, intuitives don't like routine, and prefer ideas.

The third scale is **thinking** compared to **feeling.** What do you do when you have gathered your facts and impressions? A thinking person will base their judgements more on impersonal analysis and logic than on personal values, whereas a feeling person will base judgements more on personal values.

Finally, the fourth scale looks at **judging** as opposed to **perceiving**. The judging attitude probably means you like a planned, decided, orderly way of life, more than a flexible and spontaneous way. The opposite of this is a perceptive attitude which probably means you like a flexible, spontaneous way of life better than a planned, decided or orderly way. This scale also separates those who value being well organised and structured, from those who thrive on ambiguity.

Myers Briggs tends to emphasise the positive side of your nature and can be very helpful in understanding your strengths. Many managers tend to be either types ESTJ (extrovert, sensing, thinking, judging) or ENTJ (extrovert, intuitive, thinking, judging), i.e. most of their scores are on the extrovert scale, although they can be also intuitive as well as sensing. (This suggests stereotyping, but this is not necessarily the case, as this is not how Myers Briggs is used; you can be a successful manager and not be one of these types.)

The Myers Briggs Type Indicator provides brief descriptions of each type. However, whatever your preferences, you may still use some behaviours characteristic of contrasting preferences, especially when a preference is low. For example, a person who is type ESTJ is described as 'practical, realistic, matter of fact, with a natural head for business. Not interested in subjects they see no use for, but can apply themselves when necessary. Like to organise and run activities, may make good administrators especially if they remember to consider others' feelings and points of view'.

The opposite to ESTJ would be INFP, who would be described as 'full of enthusiasms and loyalties, but they seldom talk of these until they know you well. Care about learning, ideas, language and independent projects of their own. Tend to undertake too much then somehow get it done. Friendly, but often too absorbed in what they are doing to be sociable. Little concerned with possessions or physical surroundings'.

Each of the types are analysed in more detail in the feedback session and this is matched to the **work scene.** For example, ESTJs tend to be logical, analytical, decisive and tough minded, and are able to organise facts and operations well in advance. ESTJs make useful contributions to an organisation, in terms of seeing flaws in advance, being able to critique programmes in a logical way, being able to organise the process, product and people, able to monitor to see if the job is done and able to follow through in a step-by-step way.

The **leadership style** of a typical ESTJ is to seek leadership directly and take charge quickly, apply and adapt past experiences to solve problems, be crisp and direct at getting to the core of the situation, be quick to decide, act as a traditional leader who respects the hierarchy. ESTJs preferred work environment contains hard-working people focused on getting the job done, is task-oriented, organised and structured, provides stability and predictability, is focused on efficiency and rewards the meeting of goals.

The **potential pitfalls** which face the ESTJ include the possibility that they may decide too quickly, they may not see the need for change, they may overlook the niceties in working to get the job done, and may be overtaken by their feelings and values if they ignore them for too long. ESTJs should consider all sides before deciding, including the human element, may need to prod themselves to look at the benefits of change, may need to make a special effort to show appreciation of others, and may need to take time to reflect and identify their feelings and values.

Value to the employer/user

Myers Briggs looks in detail at the preferences an individual has, and identifies a particular personality type which can be a focus for discussion in management development, team-building and occasionally selection. It can sometimes be difficult for one Myers Briggs type to understand others' viewpoints and this type indicator can be helpful in team-building, and helping specific types to come to terms with others' strengths and weaknesses.

Some organisations have developed a particular enthusiasm for Myers Briggs and use it extensively on people coming into their organisation, and in matching people to specific tasks.

Value to the employee/ person being tested

It can be very helpful for an individual to explore their own preferences, and become aware of their strengths and their particular development needs. When you understand the different Myers Briggs types, it becomes a very useful way of understanding the personalities of the people around you. It can be possible to guess at it, but we are not always aware of someone's true type. It certainly helps to see yourself in context more effectively, and to know your strengths and weaknesses in a more readily understandable form than some of the other basic personality tests offer.

Value to the user organisation

Myers Briggs types can be readily matched with corporate culture types, and can be mixed and matched in team groups. In some organisations certain 'types' may be more frequently represented in certain roles but it is important to remember that different types can complement each other and stereotyping is to be avoided.

Can the test results be deliberately falsified?

It would be difficult to falsify Myers Briggs results, because the questions and the choices are quite subtle, and do not appear to be directly related to specific personality types.

Advantages over other tests

Myers Briggs produces clearly-defined types, and discussion allows subtle differences to be explained, which can be used to analyse most people effectively. It is well respected and particularly user-friendly.

Disadvantages compared with other tests

If not used appropriately, Myers Briggs does tend to slot people into one of the 16 types without much leeway, and clearly people are more different and diverse than this. It requires some sympathy with, and understanding for, the underlying psychology, and not everyone has this. However, it should be emphasised that it is recognised that everyone is different, and Myers Briggs looks at 'preference' and should not be used categorically to pigeon-hole people. There should always be discussion about the preference scores and what they mean.

Tests may be combined with . . .

Can be used on its own, but could also be used with other measures to gain a fuller picture. Could be combined, for example, with GMA Abstract and Raven's Progressive Matrices to test strategic thinking, especially for ESTJ and ENTJ types being selected for senior management.

Static/predictive value

Myers Briggs provides a useful present picture of the individual, and is indicative of how people are likely to behave in given situations, based on the appropriate personality type.

Overall review

Speed of being tested – fast
Speed of scoring results – fast
Cost – low
Range of applications – wide
In-house/Out-house – In-house, under licence
Basic/Advanced – basic

How to prepare yourself for sitting this test

It should be borne in mind that the Myers Briggs Type Indicator aims to define personality types based on an individual's responses to a series of statements, and includes questions which deal overall with the way you like to use your perception and judgement, i.e. the way you like to look at things and the way you like to go about deciding things. It is best just to 'be yourself', and any subtleties which do not come through in the test can be brought up in the discussion.

Will this test produce a different result after a period of time?

Unlikely, unless you have undergone a total change of career, or if you are still developing your preferences in these areas.

16-PF

Background

16-PF (16 personality factors) is also a very popular, fairly quick-to-use inventory. The Industrial Society, in their guide to assessment and selection, rated the 16-PF most highly relevant among the many personality questionnaires which have been successfully developed for use with normal populations, and which have shown promise in personnel selection. (They also mentioned the Guildford-Zimmerman Temperament Survey, the Gordon Personal Profile Inventory, the Myers Briggs Type Indicator, the OPQ and the Managerial and Professional Profiler.)

As a model of personality types, 16-PF has rapidly become well accepted in the psychometric field, and is one of the most well-known standard tests. Devised by Cattell from 1946–9, the 16-PF is based around the proposal that an individual's personality consists of 16 different personality factors, a conclusion which was also based on the application of factor analysis to statements about the individual's personality. The test is now published by NFER Nelson.

More and more validation studies have been carried out, with a number of normative groups now developed. The large amount of normative data available adds considerably to the value of 16-PF.

This personality questionnaire, based on the first Cattell model, but considerably refined over the years, has provided a profile of the individual's personality which has given a far more sophisticated picture than the first simple Eysenck model (described in the Introduction) would provide. There are several textbooks and learned treatises on each of these different personality types. This test, used prescriptively, looks at combinations of personality types and provides a picture of the individual, combining 16 unrelated factors.

The aims of the test

The 16-PF can be used, among other applications, for identifying personalities which fit specific profiles for occupational applications. For example, it would be possible to identify a sales person profile, a manager profile, a researcher profile and a number of other profiles which can be matched against individuals.

There can be some inherent contradictions in 16-PF and it is necessary to carry out extensive feedback to find out what is driving the person, in order to explain the personality type into which they seem to fit most appropriately.

Some people come over as very aggressive or authoritarian in 16-PF, as it tends to show up extremes of personality rather than giving a rounded picture. The test has been normed extensively over many years, but it still tends to show bi-polar results.

The format

16-PF includes a list of just over 100 statements on a self-scoring sheet. In completing 16-PF, it is simply a case of choosing between two statements given, with the option also to choose a midway answer. Thus there are three options to each statement. In the instructions, the testee is asked to choose the first natural answer which comes into their minds and not opt for the in-between option too often, perhaps only every four or five times.

Range of applications

Mostly used in selection procedures, in middle and senior management, but can be used at other levels too.

Doing the test

This test takes about half an hour to complete, longer than PAPI, for example, because there are basically more options to choose from, with the three possible answers of yes, in between, and no; true, in between, false; and yes, sometimes, no.

The 100+ questions are simple and straightforward, and it is relatively easy to choose between them. One problem can be the fact that, if the testees are familiar with the idea of doing tests with only two options, it is easy to forget that the third option of 'in between' is available. It is open to dispute as to whether or not the instruction to choose the in-between option no more than every four or five times is a good idea.

Examples of content of the test

A typical 16-PF question might be 'Money can't buy happiness?' to be answered by opting for true, in between, or false. The 16-PF also includes a number of logical reasoning tests such as 'Adult is to child as cat is to . . .?'

Apart from these, there are always three options accompanying every question. They are all of general application and are not work-related.

Time needed to complete the test

About 30 minutes.

Time to score the test

About 10–15 minutes on the self-scoring sheet.

Necessary time for feedback

Often about 20–30 minutes, but may vary depending on the objectives of the feedback.

Format/structure of the feedback

In the feedback, the 16-PF results are then related specifically to personality characteristics, which have been very well validated. The 16-PF results can be examined in some depth to produce a detailed report, or can be used just to create a quick profile. There are also a number of second order factors, which can be looked at in more detail. The 16-PF, as the name suggests, examines personality types according to 16 personality factors, and is also useful for analysing stress levels and anxiety.

16-PF is not specifically work-related, and gives indications of general personality type. Details of the implications of this for the work environment can be explored in the feedback. Some of the descriptions in the 16-PF are quite negative, yet it can be useful in the structuring of an interview, and in looking at reasons for success or failure in a given workplace.

The second order factors can be looked at in more detail, and males and females can be scored slightly differently.

Value to the employer/user

The 16-PF is one of the most well-known tests and can be very popular on a long-term basis. Some companies use it without other tests and without discussion, which is probably not advisable. 16-PF provides a good, basic personality description which is of value as a general tool for use in interviews for selection, and sometimes for career development and team-building. It can be useful for comparing one person with other employees.

Value to the employee/person being tested

16-PF is most useful when the person being tested is given the opportunity to discuss it in feedback sessions. The results can then be fully explained in the context of the occupational environment. It can form an interesting insight into the factors which make up personalities, and can be especially useful to someone who has not completed a personality test before.

Value to the user organisation

16-PF types can be linked to particular corporate cultures, especially relating to the amount of risk required in operating in a certain corporate environment. They can be compared with Belbin and used for team-building, when used in combination with OPQ and other more occupationally-oriented tests.

Can the test results be deliberately falsified?

There is a concern that the 16-PF is easier to falsify than some other tests, which can be a problem because it is extensively used in selection. By contrast, it is hard to fake PAPI, because of the element of forced choice. However, the basic personality type can be revealed during the feedback, which would show up any attempts to falsify it.

Advantages over other tests

16-PF offers a more in-depth discussion than a number of other basic personality tests, and it is well established with extensive norm groups, in contrast with some of the newer tests.

Disadvantages compared with other tests

The 16-PF is very well established as one of the traditional questionnaires, but – as with other instruments – used incorrectly it can be almost dangerous, and it most certainly needs feedback discussion. There are some strict guidelines as to training in the use of 16-PF, but these are not always adhered to and it can get diluted in value. The 16-PF does not appear to have immediate occupational value, because it is not specifically geared towards the workplace.

Tests may be combined with . . .

16-PF may be combined with other personality type indicators, such as the Myers Briggs or OPQ, to gather more in-depth information, or PAPI to look at how the personality is seen in the individual's workstyle.

Static/predictive value

Good static value of personality type, and useful for predicting behaviour, especially in teams.

Overall review

Speed of being tested – moderate
Speed of scoring results – moderate
Cost – low
Range of applications – especially selection
In-house/Out-house – In-house
Basic/Advanced – basic

How to prepare yourself for sitting this test

The questions are very general, and easy to complete, and the only way to answer them is with an entirely open mind, without necessarily thinking of the implications of any of the answers. It is very straightforward and does not need intellectual inputs.

Will this test produce a different result after a period of time?

Possibly, but not often, as the basic personality type revealed by 16-PF will not change radically over time.

The OPQ 4.2

Background

The OPQ (Occupational Personality Questionnaire) was designed by, and is published by, Saville & Holdsworth (SHL), the UK market leaders in occupational psychometric tests. There are a variety of versions of OPQ, ranging from the quite simple to the more sophisticated. The most popular OPQ versions are for senior and middle management, and these include Concept 4.2 (reviewed here). Other very popular models are Concepts 3 and 5.2 (although Concept 3 is now being used less). These personality questionnaires analyse the typical behaviour of individuals in an occupational setting, and also have some input on the behaviour of individuals in groups.

The early versions of the OPQ were devised in the early 1980s to be effective over a variety of occupations at middle and senior level. At this point, Saville & Holdsworth comprised just two people, its eponymous founders. The company now includes 50 psychologists, with approximately 150 staff in the UK, based at a large training centre at Long Ditton, with the main centre in Thames Ditton, Surrey. The company holds open days, describing and demonstrating the personality tests for potential customers.

The OPQ tests can be used directly through Saville & Holdsworth, or under licence (which limits the extent of usage to trained users only, who can test as many people as they like). In promoting their tests, SHL has invited celebrities like Richard Branson and Sir John Harvey-Jones to complete a normal OPQ exercise.

Saville & Holdsworth have worldwide rights on a number of personality questionnaires. These were mostly used in the past for selection purposes and are now also used for career development. OPQ is one of the most well-known of Saville & Holdworth's range of instruments, which includes very many others for a variety of purposes, including ability tests, often in a number of languages.

The aims of the test

OPQ are basic personality tests which aim to present a fuller picture of the individual than others on the market, while at the same time being user-friendly and being clearly understandable by the non-specialist. To a certain extent, Saville & Holdsworth have succeeded, and the OPQ tests are popular with many employers, executive search consultants and outplacement firms. OPQ Concept 4.2 is expected to be current for the next 5 years, and through its 30 different dimensions of personality, has proved itself to be very useful in selection. It is seen as highly job-relevant when incorporated with a job analysis.

The format

In the Concept 4.2 questionnaire, the testee is presented with blocks of statements in four parts, marked a), b), c) and d). Testees choose the statement which is most true or typical of their everyday behaviour, and then the opposite, that which is least true. If the test is being completed manually and the choices indicated on the answer sheet provided, the testee fills in the appropriate circle marked 'most' and then fills in the circle marked 'least'.

For example, take these four statements:

a) is assertive in groups,
b) applies common sense,
c) can sell ideas to a customer,
d) manages to relax easily.

The testee is asked to decide which statement is the most appropriate to them, and which is the least appropriate. The test can also be done on a computer by indicating options as they come up on a screen by pressing specified keys. This produces a scored result more quickly, including an expert system report of 11 pages in a few moments.

Range of applications

Across a wide range of junior, middle and senior management functions.

Doing the test

In Concept 4.2, the person being tested is asked to think about each particular statement and is then scored according to a certain norm group. It is an ipsitive test (see Glossary), in so far as the testee analyses most preferred and least preferred statements, prioritising most and least. (There is a certain similarity with the PAPI test here.)

The testee is asked to be very careful that the question number on the answer sheet corresponds to the question booklet. When completed by computer, the testee must be sure that they have indicated their desired choice (there is a correcting mechanism if a mistake is made).

The person being tested is asked to be as discerning and honest as possible, and not to give a certain response just because it seems the right thing to say, or it is how you might like it to be.

Saville & Holdsworth mention that they appreciate that, in some statement blocks, the statements may not be very relevant and it may be difficult to choose which are the most appropriate in order to answer the questions, but a decision must be made in each case. It is vital to complete all the questions and the testee should work fairly quickly without pondering at length over any one question.

Examples of content of the test

(Not possible for copyright reasons.)

Time needed to complete the test

About 30–40 minutes.

Time to score the test

By computer, about five minutes. Concept 4.2 can only be administered and scored using a PC or hand-held computer, while other concept versions can be hand-scored, taking somewhat longer.

Necessary time for feedback

At least 30 minutes, ideally 1 hour.

Format/structure of the feedback

The profile chart relating to the Concept 4.2 test analyses the profile of the testee according to three main sectors: relationships, thinking style and feelings:

within **relationships,** the profile considers whether the testee is assertive, is gregarious and/or has empathy;

under **thinking style,** the test looks at fields of use, abstract and structure;

under **feelings and emotions** the profile examines anxieties, controls and energies.

This produces a profile with 30 measures of personality and also looks at the consistency of the responses as a check.

The profile measures preferences according to a 'stens' scale, a psychologist's term for measuring preference strength.

The OPQ also looks at **team types** and **leadership styles**. Under team types, the profile defines the extent to which the testee is one of the following eight types (based on the Belbin model): co-ordinator, shaper, plant, monitor/evaluator, resource investigator, completer, team worker and implementer.

Among 'leadership styles', the report looks at five types: directive leader, delegative leader, participative leader, consultative leader and negotiative leader.

The profile also considers the individual's degree of adaptability.

The OPQ also looks at **subordinate styles** under five headings: receptive subordinate, self-reliant subordinate, collaborative subordinate, informative subordinate and reciprocating subordinate.

These profiles are presented along a stens scale of 1 to 10, according to the appropriateness of each.

The expert report, printed out from a computer-scoring process and given to the person being tested, reiterates the profile chart and presents a short narrative analysing the main points of the profile in more detail. This is followed by a full report looking at relationships, thinking style, feelings and emotions. The Saville & Holdsworth norm was, in this instance, a large, mixed group, all of whom have tackled these 100 questions over the last few years.

Whitehead Mann Audit & Assessment have developed a new OPQ norm, defined as a senior managerial group. This norm includes far more senior people than that used by Saville & Holdsworth, which tends to consist of a widely-defined graduate and middle management group. Whitehead Mann use OPQ 4.2 extensively, and have built up a series of alternative norms, including one based on a group of professional women. There are significantly different ways of assessing testees, according to their occupational and seniority norms, and this certainly affects the validity of the test.

Whitehead Mann have developed a series of high-level norms which show typical characteristics of particularly high-achieving people. High-level managers tend to be controlling and planning, and are driven by the exercise of power; they also tend to be more forward-thinking than average (lower-level managers tend to work in a more immediate and less planned way).

It is essential that people being tested should be normed against the right peer group, otherwise their characteristics which would appear average against their appropriate norm would be exaggerated in the basic norm. Thus, the norms chosen are very important, and the standard Saville & Holdsworth norm, scored against a large, professional graduate group, can give a different reading when the same results are scored against different norms. For example, a person tested in relation to Saville & Holdsworth's norms was shown to be more ambitious and forward planning than the lower level norms, and was much more typical of higher level managers. As an experiment, a standard Saville & Holdsworth norm was compared with a high managerial norm and a high-level female norm. How were they different?

The same person being tested appeared to be much more persuasive in the basic norm than against the high-level norms. The same person was less controlling in the basic norm. She was more independent in the basic norm, less outgoing and less affiliative. Her level of social confidence was about the same in each. Modesty was lower in the high-level female norm. Being democratic scored lower in the high-level norms. Being practical scored higher in the high-level norms. Being data rational was lower in the basic norms. Behavioural and conceptual thinking were much lower in the high-level female norm group. Forward planning was higher in the basic norms. Critical feelings were higher in the basic norms, but competitiveness was lower in the high-level managerial norms. Being achievement-oriented and being decisive were higher in the basic norms.

What does all this mean? The basic norms will indicate greater extremes, if the person is very much more achievement-oriented, conscientious and persuasive than the large professional and graduate norm. In comparison with a high-level management norm, persuasiveness will be less extreme, and so will innovativeness and being achievement-oriented. It is much more usual for a high-level management group to be more persuasive, more innovative, more critical and more achieving than a general management norm.

In the high-level female norm, where certain characteristics tend to be emphasised, there were other specific differences. There are differences from the high-level management norm: the latter shows less independence, less modesty, more practical thinking, more of an artistic nature, more behavioural thought, less conceptual thinking, more forward planning, more worrying, less tough-mindedness, less competitiveness and more achievement orientation.

Thus, the female norms show that this person is more competitive than the norm, more tough-minded, more innovative and more practical. However, she is less modest, and less behavioural in thinking, and less conceptual than typical high-level females.

These differences between norms are not particularly great, but they are significant, and again it should be stressed that it is important to be normed against your representative group as accurately as possible. It is unusual for the variants to be more than one or two stens (points on the scale) different, but where this occurs, such as where a person is very highly achievement-oriented against basic norms, yet considerably lower against exact norms – in this case high-level female – the differences are obviously quite important.

Against the same high-level norms, it is possible to classify a person according to their **selling styles** profile chart. This chart looks at the extent to which a person is product or people-oriented in their sales approach and the degree to which they are adaptable. Are they likely to perceive different requirements in different situations?

It is also possible to use the OPQ to analyse **behavioural styles,** and again, this is most appropriate against the most relevant norm group. OPQ behavioural styles include:

confident communicator, a person who copes well in formal situations;

rapport creator, who quickly builds warm and friendly relationships;

culture fitter who identifies and fits the prevailing customer culture;

culture breaker, a person valued for new ideas against the prevailing culture;

enthusiast, who infects customers with energetic enthusiasm;

perseverers, who succeed by determined persistence to achieve a sale;

business winners, who strive for success in a competitive situation and thrive on competition;

technicians, who enjoy a technical style of selling;

administrative supporters, who reassure customers who feel a need to be assured of administrative quality; and

team managers, who understand how to assign, motivate and advise.

The OPQ selling styles also analyse the extent to which a person sells from the basis of interpersonal strengths and building a relationship, their energy base, and their level of energy and enthusiasm, and their thinking base and the degree to which they are rational. It is also possible to gain an idea of the extent to which the person is good in a general sales mode and is able to sell in a variety of different ways. As mentioned above, the OPQ can also be linked to Belbin Team Types.

The OPQ is widely seen as a very powerful instrument, and if it is interpreted well it is far from superficial. The OPQ is capable of great insight and can be one of the most useful one-off tests. A great many top psychologists use OPQ and, if used in a large validation study or linked to job analysis, it can be quite intricate. However, Saville & Holdworth's computer-generated summaries do not necessarily adequately replace individual, face-to-face feedback from a competent psychologist.

The real skill of OPQ interpretation is in the linking of the basic scales to give clearer insight into behaviour and to produce team-types or a user's own desired combinations. The quality of interpretation of Saville & Holdsworth's OPQ when licensed out is inevitably not universally good and poor interpretation has occasionally damaged the reputation of the instrument. Saville & Holdworth's Expert System can be mechanistic and bland, especially in the case of a person who shows few extremes in their occupational personality.

Value to the employer/user

As indicated, the OPQ can be an extremely useful general personality test for selection purposes, and can be used on its own (although with interviews and non-psychometric ways of assessment). It gains in value through more extensive use in a particular company. It is one of the most reliable and useful tests for a company with only a limited need for testing, and which does not necessarily want to develop an extensive battery of tests.

Value to the employee/person being tested

Like PAPI, the OPQ tests are becoming the most popular tests in most widespread use, and having completed it once, the testee will be reasonably well prepared for other tests in the future. The OPQ helps people to become familiar with a wide range of testing concepts, including Belbin Team Types. The OPQ helps in a preliminary understanding of workstyle and approach, and strengths and weaknesses in a corporate setting. In this respect, it is appropriate for people going through outplacement and preparing CVs.

Value to the user organisation

The OPQ can help significantly in selecting people for appropriate corporate cultures, and in team-building. The results are in sufficient detail, in terms of workstyle and occupational characteristics, to predict the success or failure of certain individuals in certain organisations. Those who are sufficiently self-reliant and individualistic to succeed in macho cultures are clearly apparent, as are those able to cope with the work pace of retail cultures. Personalities most suited for process cultures on the one hand, and high-risk slow-feedback cultures on the other hand, will be visible in a quantifiable way, to a greater extent than in more basic personality tests, even PAPI.

Can the test results be deliberately falsified?

With difficulty, because many of the statements do not appear to bear close relation to the personality types being analysed, and trying to slant the answers in a certain way would be difficult to sustain. Also, in Concept 4.2, you often have to choose 'most' and 'least' from four options which have apparently similar 'social desirability' or attractiveness.

Advantages over other tests

More detail, wider scope than more basic tests. Can be used successfully on its own. Extensive norm groups are being developed, both for UK and many other countries.

Disadvantages compared with other tests

Can be seen to be superficial by a small minority of purist psychologists, but these are now few and far between. OPQ also depends heavily on competent test administration and feedback. Attempts to produce computer-generated feedback have been widely criticised by some.

Tests may be combined with . . .

Can be used with more specific tests, such as Sweney's, Fleishman's and Thomas-Kilman, and with conceptual-thinking tests. Or can be used on its own. It can be combined with Saville & Holdsworth ability tests like the Management and Graduate Item Bank.

Static/predictive value

Good indicator of outlook of person, also useful in predicting behaviour in leadership or subordinate role, or in teams. Likely to be valid as a predictor for at least a year.

Overall review

Speed of being tested – moderately fast
Speed of scoring results – fast by computer

Cost – low to medium
Range of applications – wide
In-house/Out-house – Out-house at SHL, In-house under licence
Basic/Advanced – basic (but can have advanced applications)

How to prepare yourself for sitting this test

Make sure that the instructions are fully understood, and that you
are thinking in a working context, rather than socially. Be
prepared to have to make decisions and choices which may not
exactly express how you feel.

Will this test produce a different result after a period of time?

Possibly, and companies using the OPQ extensively will expect to
be able to use an OPQ result for only about 1 year to 18 months.
You will be asked if you have completed an OPQ before, and how
long ago; if this was more than 1 year or 18 months, the probability
is that you will be asked to repeat it.

FIRO-B

Background

This questionnaire, originally developed just before the Second World War, was at first used for assessing US armed services recruits. Designed by Will Schutz Ph.D, FIRO-B dates back to 1958 and the most recent version was copyrighted in 1987. The latest version is known as 'Elements of Awareness – B'. The impetus for developing the theory and the questionnaires was obtained during Schutz's work at the US Naval Research Laboratory in 1952, in helping understand people working and living together on board ships and submarines.

The range of FIRO questionnaires includes FIRO-B for behaviour (discussed below), FIRO-BC for children's behaviour, FIRO-F for feeling, COPE (Coping Operations Preference Enquiry), looking at people's defence mechanisms in anxiety-provoking interpersonal situations, LIPHE (Life Interpersonal History Enquiry), looking at people's behaviour and feelings towards their parents, and VAL-ED (Education Values), looking at the values a person holds about an educational situation.

The latest – and now increasingly popular – version is Elements of Awareness B, which overlaps but extends FIRO-B. FIRO-B examines a person's expressed behaviour but not what he or she wants to express. It examines what a person wants to get, but not what he or she actually gets. Elements of Awareness extends this.

The aims of the test

FIRO-B is designed to help people to become more aware of how they behave towards other people, and how other people behave towards them. The test revolves around three concepts:

being **included**, i.e. doing things with other people, and sharing;

controlling, i.e. taking charge and influencing;

openness, i.e. disclosing and telling true feelings.

Schutz's original idea was based around examining the difference between your reality as you perceive it, and what you would really like to be and to have. In the FIRO-B test, you are asked to identify what you see as your reality, and then reappraise the questions according to what you would like to be true in your case.

This questionnaire is therefore useful in analysing personal degrees of control, and tensions which may exist in people. It shows a difference between how things are perceived and how you would like them to be, especially in terms of your relationships with people, in the basic concepts of including, controlling and openness.

The FIRO-B does not 'measure' anything, but the scores estimate the levels of behaviour with which unique individuals feel comfortable, or 'correct', in relation to each person's needs for inclusion, control and affection.

Schutz, in developing the FIRO-B, observed that much of the behaviour that is exhibited towards others is motivated by differing levels of needs for these three interpersonal dimensions, and research has substantiated their importance in human interaction.

The format

The intention of FIRO-B is to look at each of 54 statements in both ways separately, i.e. as 'what I see' and 'what I want'. The 54 statements are listed in the centre of the self-scoring form, with 'what I see' on the left-hand side, and 'what I want' on the right.

FIRO-B is designed to analyse the three dimensions of include, control and open. To what extent do you include others in your plan and do you wish to be included in groups? To what extent do you exert control over your feelings? To what extent do you control what you do and how you behave? How open are you with superiors, colleagues and subordinates? The questionnaire gives a series of scores relating to a person's profile, in terms of how they see themselves, and their dissatisfaction with their wanted behaviour.

Range of applications

Since 1958, according to the FIRO-B accompanying literature, thousands of people have used the FIRO-B, including managers at all levels in virtually every type of business. FIRO-B is also used extensively in clinical psychology, with married couples, union workers, entrepreneurs, students, teachers, ministers, military personnel, politicians, police officers, firemen, doctors, lawyers and many others, from all walks of life.

Doing the test

The testee must go through each statement systematically and consider to what extent this statement expresses reality for them, and indicate this on the left-hand side of the self-scoring sheet. This is the testee's perception of what they think is true. The testee is then asked to reappraise each statement according to whether or not they would want this to be true. It is important to avoid the temptation to look at each statement in turn, decide if it is true and then if it is what you want.

Examples of content of the test

'I seek out people to be with'
'I am totally honest with close friends'
'I am the dominant person when I am with people'
'People include me in their activities'
'People decide things for me'
'I strongly influence other people's ideas'
'When people are doing things together I join them'
'There is a part of myself I keep private'
'At least two of my friends tell me their true feelings'
'I participate in group activities'

Time needed to complete the test

This test takes about 10–15 minutes on a self-scoring sheet.

Time to score the test

Designed to be self-scored, and is quickly analysed.

Necessary time for feedback

Can be around an hour, but can be shorter. At least 20–30 minutes would be necessary.

Format/structure of the feedback

The 12 scores, relating to the 6 variables according to the actual profile and dissatisfaction, range from 0–9, with the score indicating the degree to which the person agrees with the statement. The scores are a reflection of how the person has chosen to be and to behave, up to now. It is emphasised in the FIRO-B scoring that the person has the ability to change, according to their desire and willingness to learn to change. The FIRO-B feedback suggests that if people find themselves responding angrily or defensively to one of the scores it could be that they believe, deep down inside, that the score is accurate and yet they do not want it to be.

The first part of the interpretation looks at the degree to which the person already **includes** other people in their life, and the degree to which they want to include people. They may be dissatisfied in terms of including more people than they want to, and wanting to include people more than they already do. The basis of FIRO-B is the indication of dissatisfaction, and a discrepancy between the perceived needs and what is already achieved.

The second part of the profile analysis looks at how the person perceives **they are included** by other people in their activities. To what extent do people include me? To what extent do I want people to include me? Elements of dissatisfaction are shown in whether or not the person completing the test considers that people include them more than they want them to, or if the person wants them to include them more than they do already. The scores in each case show the extent of the discrepancy.

In the third element of the interpretation the degree of **control** of other people is analysed. Do I control people, and do I want to control people? The degree of dissatisfaction is shown in terms of 'I control people more than I want to', and 'I want to control people more than I do'.

The fourth element of the profile looks at the extent to which the person feels that **they are controlled** by other people and how much they want people to control them. They can be dissatisfied in so far as they are controlled by people more than they want them to, and if they want people to control them more than they do.

The final two interpretation elements are about openness. To what extent am I **open** with people? To what extent do I want to be open with people? On the negative side, a person can be more open with people than they want to be, and can want to be more open with people than they are already. In the last interpretative element, the person responding to the instrument considers whether or not **people are open with me?**, and if I want people to be open with me. On the dissatisfaction scale it can be concluded whether or not the person feels that 'People are open with me more than I want them to be' or 'I want people to be open with me more than they are'.

So, at the basis of FIRO-B is the division of each interpersonal dimension into:

a) what behaviour is seen to be most comfortable, and is most commonly exhibited towards other people; and
b) what behaviour is felt to be required in relationships with other people.

The FIRO-B test divides each interpersonal dimension into two elements:

expressed behaviour, or how individuals believe they behave toward others; and

wanted behaviour, or how individuals want others to behave towards them.

Therefore, each individual will show either expressed or wanted behaviour for inclusion, control and affection.

The expressed aspect of each dimension relates to aspects of behaviour seen as most comfortable in using towards others to bring people together (referred to as 'expressed inclusion'), in order to get our own way in what we want ('expressed control') and what we feel is the most appropriate to be close to others ('expressed affection').

On the other hand, the wanted element of each dimension of behaviour refers to how we want others to treat us in their attitude towards relationships with us ('wanted inclusion'), to get their way ('wanted control') and to be close in their relationship to us ('wanted affection').

'**Expressed inclusion**' means that we want to include other people in our way of life at work or socially and be included in theirs. This also means we want to belong to social or work groups and have the company of other people as much as possible.

'**Expressed control**' refers to trying to exert control and influence over things, to taking charge of things and telling other people what to do.

'**Expressed affection**' means that we try to become close to people, that we express friendliness and try to show personal warmth in relationships.

'**Wanted inclusion**' means that we tend to want other people to include us in their activities and to invite us to belong, even if we do not make much of an effort to be included.

'**Wanted control**' refers to us needing others to control us and wanting others to influence us, and sometimes even tell us what to do.

'**Wanted affection**' defines feelings of wanting others to express friendliness and personal warmth towards us, and wanting others to be close to us.

According to Ed Musselwhite, in a pamphlet describing the interpretation of FIRO-B results, published by the Consulting Psychologists Press of California, this test helps in understanding individual levels of needs with respect to the interpersonal dimensions. We have a sense that 'all is right in our interpersonal world' when our needs are met in our relationships at about the levels that we view as 'correct' and comfortable for ourselves, based on our unique life experiences.

If we experience more than our preferred, comfortable level of one or more of these dimensions, we may feel we're being crowded, pushed, or smothered. If we experience less than our preferred, comfortable level of one or more of these dimensions, we may have feelings of being left out, of being without proper direction, or of being rejected, unloved or unappreciated.

Individual FIRO-B scores can vary dramatically on most dimensions and elements; some people being tested will have almost all low scores; some will have mixed high, low and middle-range scores; and some have scores near the middle of the range for almost all dimensions.

Needs for each 'interpersonal dimension' can be seen as an important personal preference within relationships. There is a tendency to fall into a blaming, attacking or retreating role with others when a preferred level of need is not being met. This can be coped with if it is possible to understand why a person is behaving in this way. 'Rather than adjusting our interactions to try to reach our preferred level, we may instead take a one-up or one-down posture toward those who aren't "doing right" by us. Such posturing rarely succeeds; most often it drives wedges between ourselves and others and makes it even more difficult for us to get our needs met', explains Musselwhite in the FIRO-B interpretation pamphlet.

'Unless we have some understanding of what we want from others in regard to the three dimensions, it is all too easy to miss important opportunities to build and maintain relationships that could be satisfying for everyone concerned. When things are going well, we may be pleased, but unclear about how we got there; when things are going badly, we may not have a meaningful awareness of what has changed or how to go about creating the good times again.'

A closer view of inclusion, control and affection, and their expressed and wanted aspects is explained in the feedback session, as each person's FIRO-B scores are estimates of 'how much' each interpersonal dimension seems comfortable for each person.

In the feedback session, the person doing the test can be asked additional questions, according to 'how much' they consider each of a series of questions to be relevant.

Expressed inclusion

How much do I include others in activities or ideas?

How much do I do to get myself included in activities or ideas?

How much do I create opportunities for people to be with me at social occasions or meetings?

How much do I create togetherness?

How much do I demonstrate team-building or people-connecting behaviour?

How much do I demonstrate a sense of community in my behaviour?

Wanted inclusion

How much do I want to be included by others in activities or ideas?

How much do I want to be an invited guest or participant at a meeting?

How much do I want togetherness?

How much do I want to be a team player?

How much do I want to be part of a community or a network of people?

Expressed control

How much do I take charge, directly or indirectly?

How much do I work at getting my way, through my position, influence or charisma?

How much do I exercise power?

How much do I 'put myself in the driver's seat'?

How much do I direct the actions or ideas of others?

Wanted control

How much do I want others to take charge?

How much do I want others to get their way?

How much do I want other people to tell me what to do?

How much do I want others to 'be in the driver's seat'?

How much do I want my actions or my ideas directed by others?

Expressed affection

How much do I initiate close personal relationships with others?

How much do I invite others to deepen their personal relationships with me?

How much do I share about myself with others?

How much closeness to others do I demonstrate?

How much do I risk in my attempts to reach out to others?

Wanted affection

How much do I want close relationships with others?

How much do I want to deepen their personal relationships with me?

How much do I want others to share with me about themselves?
How much closeness do I want from others?
How much risk do I want others to take in their attempts to
reach out to me?

Some of these other questions overlap, and other questions could
be added to them. But the person administering the test may use
these as additional contexts to help you understand your FIRO-B
scores.

The newest version of FIRO-B, Elements of Awareness B, adds
to the study of aspects of behaviour looked at in the traditional
FIRO-B model. For instance, FIRO-B looks at expressed
behaviour but not at what is wanted to be expressed, and at what
people want to get but not at what they do get. Thus, FIRO-B
looks at inclusion from the point of view of 'I include people',
control from 'I control people' and openness from 'I am open with
people'. Then it looks at aspects of wanted behaviour in terms of 'I
want people to include me', 'I want people to control me', and 'I
want people to be open with me'.

In contrast, Elements of Awareness B looks at wanted
behaviour in terms of 'I want to include people', 'I want to control
people', and 'I want to be open with people'. It also looks at what
a person actually gets: 'People include me'; 'People control me';
'People are open with me'. Thus, the latest version of FIRO-B –
Elements of Awareness B – adds significantly to the basic questionnaire. It has been summed up as the addition of two further
aspects for consideration, called 'perceived' and 'received'. It
complicates and lengthens the questionnaire but adds important
new information.

Value to the employer/user

An employer needs to know how you can work with others, both
more senior and more junior, and how you can find a way of
interacting so that you can accommodate everyone's different
preferences. FIRO-B is useful in team-building and especially in
career development exercises, in building sound relationships. It is
also used as a selection tool.

Understanding actual, perceived and preferred behaviours can
affect relationships profoundly, and these findings can be applied
with some value in a working environment.

Behaviour preferences can have significant impact on the success of interpersonal relations. The degree to which an interpersonal relationship is mutually successful tends to reflect, to a certain extent, the degree to which that relationship provides the amount of inclusion, control and affection that each person prefers. The FIRO-B helps to define these, and discrepancies can be rectified.

Value to the employee/person being tested

FIRO-B can help many of those using it to improve their understanding of how to improve their relationships with others. Clearly, this is vitally important to almost everyone and FIRO-B claims to have proven success in helping this understanding. It certainly complements other tests well, and adds quite a different dimension.

This test looks at how aware a person is in terms of the way they deal with other people. It looks at wanted behaviour compared with actual behaviour, and looks quite deeply into a field of perception which other tests do not necessarily consider. High scores indicate considerable differences between how you behave and how you want to behave.

The FIRO-B test can show someone who comes out low on affiliation and caring that they are actually more sensitive, tolerant and considerate than many people might think they are. In this sense, it is very usefully combined with more occupationally-driven tests, which may fail to emphasise this aspect.

Value to the user organisation

FIRO-B can help people to fit into specific organisations, in terms of its input on relationships. Controlling types will fit well into macho cultures, whereas including types will prefer process cultures. Open types will work well in high-risk, slow-feedback cultures. Retail (work hard/play hard) cultures tend to attract including types, and those who want to be controlled.

Can the test results be deliberately falsified?

Possibly, but the person doing the test is asked not to see the scores as judgements, but just ways of becoming more familiar with themselves. As this test is about relationships, it would be pointless to pretend to be a different type, because this would soon become obvious.

Advantages over other tests

Gives insights into relationships, and can examine feelings and sensitivities more clearly than many other tests.

Disadvantages compared with other tests

Rather American in style and rather trite in terms of the provided interpretive comments. Would need to be combined with other tests to produce a wider view, especially in the occupational context.

Tests may be combined with . . .

OPQ, Myers Briggs Type Indicator, 16-PF.

Static/predictive value

Looks at the perceptions of the individual at a given point in time, may not be so useful predictively because these could change, but useful in predicting attitudes to the specific elements of inclusion, control and openness.

Overall review

Speed of being tested – fast
Speed of scoring results – fast
Cost – low
Range of applications – wide
In-house/Out-house – In-house, under licence.
Basic/Advanced – basic

How to prepare yourself for sitting this test

No particular preparation needed, but it is worth thinking about your relationships with people at work rather than people met socially, and consider some examples of including, controlling and being open.

Will this test produce a different result after a period of time?

Possibly, if the person subsequently feels more isolated, or less, or is put into a different working environment.

GMA Abstract Test

Background

This test is part of the Graduate and Management Assessment battery published by NFER Nelson, covering abstract, numerical and verbal reasoning. This test is concerned with analysing conceptual thinking. It is an ability test rather than a personality test, but it is included here, for the same reason as Raven's Progressive Matrices, because it is used in an occupational context to analyse an ability to be visionary, to think ahead and plan for the future, a quality needed particularly among senior executives, and those in a strategic planning role. This test helps in analysing qualities relating to dealing with problems at a more abstract level.

The aims of the test

This test is designed to analyse a person's ability to handle conceptual and abstract thinking. It is easily able to show whether or not the testee prefers concrete to abstract reasoning. A person who is very successful at this test would probably make a good strategic thinker.

According to the psychologists, the GMA looks at 'fluid intelligence', 'divergent thinking', 'inductive insight' and 'flexibility of closure'. This test is based on the notion that the discovery and understanding of patterns and systems within the abstract problems is fundamental to a wide range of intellectual work, and high scores are gained by those who are able to switch easily between contexts and levels of analysis. Higher-level jobs with substantial design or strategic content often require the capacity to perceive new patterns, devise new methods and operate effectively at different levels of analysis.

People talk about someone not being able to 'see the wood for the trees'. A person who scores high on the GMA would be able to see – quite distinctly – the wood, the trees, the ecosystem, the source of timber and the recreational possibilities. The GMA Abstract Test was designed to measure these capacities with a view to identifying high-fliers.

This abstract test does not draw on educational attainment, but looks at the stages of thinking leading up to insight into the nature of a solution, rather than looking at the implementation of the solution once the principle has been discovered. Thus, it is very useful in defining an individual's ability to conceptualise, much more so than personality tests.

The format

This test is totally visual, with pictures of shapes and designs to be analysed, in boxes. There are 23 groups of tests forming each separate problem, each including 5 elements. It is necessary first to complete a series of three problems to understand how the format works, and this helps in tackling the other problems, because it is essential to become familiar with the format and what the person being tested must seek to achieve.

Range of applications

For senior management, the test is used to produce evidence of, or lack of, strategic and conceptual thinking.

Doing the test

The GMA can be found by some to be totally baffling and very difficult to complete. The problems start off easy, and then become more and more difficult. It can induce a state of panic, but this does not help and it would be better to try to settle into the way of thinking necessary to understand the problems.

This test involves studying two boxes of images. Each box is itself divided into four boxes, each containing certain shapes, mostly circles, squares, triangles and stars, with a range of other graphic designs, some outlines and some filled in as solid shapes. The testee is asked to consider these two boxes and then look at a series of five boxes below them, and decide if each of these boxes fits into either box a) type, box b) type, or neither of these.

The results can be interpreted according to the number of total problems which are correctly answered, or the number of individual boxes which were correctly ascribed among the five boxes within each problem.

It is necessary to look at each box in some detail to decide why and how they are different. Sometimes this is easy: one box may contain all squares and the other is all circles. Sometimes one box is all images which are formed from incomplete lines, whereas in others, they are all solid objects. However, in some cases it seems almost impossible to decide which box is different from the other and why.

The person being tested has been asked to sit back and look at each problem from a distance to see the whole picture, but sometimes this is easier said than done. If it is possible to decide on the principal differences between the boxes, then it is easy to choose between them. If it is impossible to decide why the boxes are different, then it seems that the only way to allocate the individual boxes is to make a decision on each one individually, mostly based on guesswork. Yet the idea is that the main theme of the boxes should be understood before the other five boxes are allocated.

The stress of completing this test satisfactorily is exacerbated by the fact that the testee is being timed and has only half an hour in which to tackle 23 problems. The person being tested is told that rather than spending too long on one particular problem, it is better to leave it and go on to the next. This makes it tempting to try and guess the answers in the hope of getting more right. However, a person with a real aptitude for conceptual thinking will not find it difficult to complete the entire test in 30 minutes, with a high degree of accuracy, based on understanding the fundamentals of each problem in turn.

Examples of content of the test

(Not possible for copyright reasons.)

Time needed to complete the test

Half an hour, strictly timed.

Time to score the test

About five minutes. The test is scored in terms of the total number of problems answered correctly, and the total elements within them which have been identified.

Necessary time for feedback

About 10–15 minutes, to explain the relevance of the findings in the context of strategic thinking within a personality appraisal, or to look at the results as part of a series of aptitude tests. Can be longer if the findings are particularly interesting. Occasionally it may be that the person being tested will have to explain why certain choices were made, and this can mean a longer feedback time.

Format/structure of the feedback

In scoring the GMA abstract test, each of the 23 problems are scored according to two criteria: either the problems are completely correct, in so far as the person taking the test has correctly chosen each of the five options within each set, or the problems are scored according to the individual correct answers to each separate option within each problem.

The marks gained are scored according to the total correct (out of 23) and the elements of each problem correct (out of 115). The percentile rank is analysed according to both. The norm group is indicated (at Whitehead Mann Audit & Assessment, this is 'managerial and professional staff'). The elements correct are referred to as 'the raw score' and the total problems correct as 'the alternative score'.

Most graduates are expected to get at least 8 problems totally correct out of the total of 23. A person who is a very concrete thinker may only get half this number, around 3 or 5, whereas a person who is good at strategic and conceptual thinking may well get twice this number right, around 16–20. It would be quite remarkable to get all the problems entirely right.

In another way of marking a test, it is possible also to analyse the number which were 80, 60, 40 or 20 per cent right. The person administering the test will explain the implications of the various scores.

The problems get progressively more difficult, so it would be expected that the first problems would be more likely to be correctly answered than the later ones, but this is not necessarily the case. Although the tests do get harder, it is possible to become more familiar with the variables of the way the problems are constructed and gain more points towards the end.

Again, it is necessary to make sure you are being normed against an appropriate group. The implications of high or low scores are then discussed in the context of the person's career. It may be that you are low on strategic and conceptual thinking, but this is quite acceptable in a goal-centred role, and in a position requiring individual attention to specific tasks. High scores would be more appropriate to a person in an important leadership position, who is required to formulate long-term strategy and offer visionary ideas, who needs to be able to think conceptually and look to the future.

Value to the employer/user

The GMA abstract test clearly analyses whether or not a person can handle abstract thinking or whether they prefer concrete concepts. How good are they at dealing with complexity? Do they like to deal with conceptual challenges?

This test is highly appropriate to senior management selection, to the problem of looking for qualities needed for corporate leadership. It is highly significant within a battery of other personality tests. In this context, it could be used without other aptitude tests, as the only 'right or wrong' test within a battery. At lower grades, it could be used within a range of tests to examine basic ability.

Value to the employee/person being tested

This test shows the ability to think conceptually and can be quite mentally stretching. It clearly indicates whether you prefer concrete or abstract thought, in a categorical way. As such, this is clearly a test rather than an indication of preference such as is typically gained through personality questionnaires. A poor result does not indicate stupidity, but less skill at tasks requiring abstract thinking.

Value to the user organisation

This test is mostly useful in matching people to role requirements, but it is also valuable in linking people to precise corporate cultures. People who are good conceptual and strategic thinkers would fit well into a high-risk, slow-feedback culture, because they would be able to plan ahead well. They would also be quite successful in macho cultures, but less so in retail and process cultures, where much of the strategic thinking is already laid down, and is less open to debate. However, not everyone in the specific culture needs to be of one type or another. Strategic thinkers are not necessary in any great number in one team, as their plans and visions can clash.

Can the test results be deliberately falsified?

Certainly not. It would be very difficult to convince the examiner of an ability in conceptual thinking if this was not present. The only way to falsify the test would be to obtain copies beforehand and learn the answers in advance. But if the test was being used to appraise suitability for a strategic role, a person's lack of strategic thinking ability would soon become obvious, even if the test had been apparently satisfactorily passed.

Advantages over other tests

Provides an opportunity to assess strategic thinking beyond that available from basic personality tests, and adds considerably to other findings in a senior management selection exercise.

Disadvantages compared with other tests

Limited to a narrow range of uses. Can cause resistance from testees unfamiliar with this type of abstract reasoning.

Tests may be combined with . . .

This test can be included within a battery of tests on verbal and numerical reasoning, but can also be combined with personality tests to provide insight on the ability to think conceptually, which can be necessary in some particular job functions and job levels.

Static/predictive value

The GMA abstract test is highly indicative of a person's ability to conceptualise at a particular point in time, and can be used to predict how they would perform in a conceptual thinking mode in an environment in which this was required.

Overall review

Speed of being tested – 30 minutes maximum
Speed of scoring results – fast
Cost – low
Range of applications – for abstract ability, conceptual thought
In-house/Out-house – In-house under licence
Basic/Advanced – more advanced

How to prepare yourself for sitting this test

There are most certainly right or wrong answers to these problems, and considerable intellectual horsepower is needed to succeed here. Therefore a high level of concentration is required, and it is best to tackle this test when you are reasonably wide awake, rather than towards the end of a busy day. You must keep trying to see the overall picture rather than being overcome by detail. Expect it to be difficult, so that if it seems easier than you expected, this will be a bonus.

Will this test produce a different result after a period of time?

It may be necessary to retake the test after several years, but the overall pattern is likely to be the same. If it was felt that the person could do better if given a second chance, then this could be done using a parallel version of the test, although scores would not, typically, be expected to change significantly.

Sweney's Decision Profile

Background

Sweney's Decision Profile was copyrighted to Arthur B. Sweney Ph.D. of Wichita, Kansas, USA in 1980. It was developed specifically to analyse the decision-making aspect of managerial and executive skills in a quick, simple and effective way. It is not yet widely used in the UK, but is employed within batteries of tests devised and arranged by Whitehead Mann Audit & Assessment.

The aims of the test

This test aims to analyse the decision-making characteristics of managers and executives, in more detail than the decision-making profiles within general occupational personality tests. It aims to define the most significant aspects of decisions, and to measure particular individuals against these, for use in selection and career development, and in team-building.

The format

Sweney's Decision Profile is produced on a single sheet listing 48 statements with true or false options. On the reverse, the decision profile can be scored according to the 13 variables.

Range of applications

For senior appointments in particular, but also for a range of general management roles, in selection and career development.

Doing the test

The test is on a self-scoring sheet, and the testee reads through each of 48 statements and indicates whether they are true or false, or questionable, in relation to one's way of deciding things, or whether they are uncertain. It is not intended that the testee should spend a long time on each one. The statements are grouped very closely together and it is easy to leave one out. It is therefore necessary to go back after the test has been completed to make sure that nothing has been omitted. The statements are straight-forward and it is relatively easy to decide between true or false. It is not advisable to opt for the questionable choice very often.

Examples of content of the test

The statements are very direct and quite American in style, and include such phrases as:

'I like for others to help me'
'I'm wild until I start winning'
'Everything I touch turns bad'
'I play hunches'

There is a clear orientation towards gambling and risk-taking in the making of decisions in this test. It is necessary for testees constantly to remind themselves that they are supposed to be answering the test according to their business experience and their job, rather than thinking about their sports or leisure activities. Those who gamble on horses or cards are naturally strongly tempted to answer the questions according to these activities, although there will be some overlap between the way they behave socially and at work.

Many of the statements relate directly to decision-making, although these are interspersed with other, more general points:

'Afterwards I wonder if my decisions are right'
'I like for others to help with risky decisions'
'I like to make fast decisions'
'My decisions are slow but usually good'
'I'm always eager to know the results of my decisions'

Many of the statements refer to luck, risk, speed, certainty and variants on these, which are not always directly related to the decision-making process.

Time needed to complete the test

About 10–15 minutes only.

Time to score the test

Can be scored by the person administering the test on the self-scoring sheet in about 10 minutes.

Necessary time for feedback

About 15–20 minutes, or more if the scores are difficult to interpret.

Format/structure of the feedback

The scoring of the decision profile is based on analysing the score of the person being tested between a low and a high ability to make effective decisions. The results are scored according to whether the person doing the test is:

- a seeker or an avoider of risk;
- if they show firm decisiveness or tend to recycle their decisions;
- whether they make independent decisions easily, or are dependent upon others;
- whether they have lucky or unlucky expectations;
- If they make fast or slow decisions;
- if they are dependent on skills for their decisions or on luck;
- if they are convinced of controlled outcomes or uncontrolled outcomes;
- if they favour hopeful perseveration of outcomes, or discouraged vacillation, tending to expect the worst;
- if they make conservative shifts in their decision, or risky shifts;
- if they make decisions based upon high risk and high gain, or low risk and low gain;
- if they use secure discipline and look to calculate risk, or decide with abandon as anxious wildness;
- if they take decisions through intuitive hunches or conscious processing.

This test asks much more than just, 'Are you decisive?', in so far as it is concerned not only with the speed of decision-making, but with the nature of decision-making. How do you calculate risk? Can you make choices easily? Are you flexible in your decisiveness? Are you confident and independent in making decisions? Do you stick to your decisions once you have made them? Are you intuitive, or do you weigh up the facts?

The test indicates whether or not someone is risk positive or negative and whether they are gamblers or not; it is possible to be risk positive but not a gambler. Some people are able to take decisions but are perhaps too cautious in doing so, yet they would fit into organisations which tend to be risk averse.

The results are scored along a rating of 10 for high and 1 for low, and in scoring the person administering the test will highlight those areas which may be particularly strong or weak.

Value to the employer/user

It may be preferable for a person to be able to take risks, to be firmly decisive, to be able to take decisions alone, to be flexible, to be optimistic, to make quick decisions, to be determined, to be disciplined and to be fully aware of the decision-making process. Alternatively, other variables may be required. This test indicates the absence or presence of these qualities, which can be exactly matched to a specific role.

Value to the employee/person being tested

This test helps in defining the attitudes to decision-making, and can highlight areas of strength and weakness which may not have been previously apparent. It is good at showing elements of pragmatism and structured decision-making. Do you tend to take gambles? Are they based on solid foundations? Do you need to be more risk-oriented than you are already? Are you too intuitive? Are you quite pessimistic, or believe you have good luck?

Value to the user organisation

This instrument is seen as particularly useful in matching individuals with corporate cultures. The nature of cultures has much to do with how a person copes with risk. For example, a person with senior responsibility in an important public utility such as a water authority might need to be a risk-averse person. However, a manager of new products would, at times, have to be more risk-oriented, and able to cope with a fairly uncertain situation. Macho and high-risk, slow-feedback cultures need a willingness to take risks, but process cultures require much less. These characteristics can be specifically used more effectively than many other tests to analyse whether or not a person would fit into one of the four Ashridge cultures of macho, process, retail (play hard/work hard), and high-risk slow-feedback (see page 14).

Can the test results be deliberately falsified?

It would be possible to appear more decisive in terms of speed of decision-making, and to use more skill than luck, but this would require an insight into the requirements of the employer, which may not be apparent. Decision-making is such an important daily task that it would be impossible to sustain a false decision-making style, so this is really not worth attempting.

Advantages over other tests

Few other instruments can provide such a detailed insight into the decision-making process. Sweney's Decision Profile is really useful in senior assessments where decision-making and risk-taking are important elements. Thus it is useful in analysing the ability of all individuals to make decisions, based on these 13 well-defined variables, looking at the decision-making process in considerably more detail than any other commonly used psychometric device. This is remarkable, given that the test itself includes only 48 statements, and is very quick and easy to complete.

Disadvantages compared with other tests

Only looks at decision-making, and therefore needs to be combined with other tests for a fuller picture, and to provide the general personality-type background. Rather American in style, and thus can sometimes be difficult for a British reader.

Tests may be combined with . . .

Sweney's Stress Index, OPQ, Myers Briggs Type Indicator.

Static/predictive value

Good at predicting how a person will react when called upon to make decisions in the future, as well as indicating present style. May not be so accurate if type of decisions to be taken varies, i.e. if they require wider responsibility or if the decisions are more important.

Overall review

Speed of being tested – fast
Speed of scoring results – fast
Cost – low
Range of applications – wide
In-house/Out-house – In-house, under licence
Basic/Advanced – basic

How to prepare yourself for sitting this test

Think about a range of decisions you have recently taken, varying from the fairly trivial to the highly significant. Consider what your approach to these decisions was. Then go through the statements and answer true or false as honestly as possible.

Will this test produce a different result after a period of time?

Possibly, if the testee has been exposed to more important levels of decision-making, and may react differently from before. A younger person may rely more on luck in decision-making, an older person more on skill. But generally, the results will be the same, because these are fundamental personality aspects.

Sweney's Stress Index

Background

Sweney's Stress Index was developed and copyrighted in the USA by V. Ann Sweney, Ph.D. and Arthur B. Sweney, Ph.D. and published by Test Systems International of Wichita, Kansas. It is one of the few instruments which specifically examines the level of stress perceived by individuals in their working and private lives. It is currently used within selected batteries of tests, particularly by Whitehead Mann Audit & Assessment.

The aims of the test

This instrument aims to measure possible causes of stress, and specifically identifies the aspects of one's daily life which are most stressful. It particularly looks at career role, financial situation, social situation and how stress is expressed in each set of circumstances. Are you always seeking approval? Are you negative about yourself? Are you optimistic or pessimistic? For each instance, expressed in a series of statements, you are asked to agree, be neutral or disagree. This is quite a straightforward test, quick to complete, which basically shows areas of potential and actual stress, and how these are coped with.

The format

The self-scoring sheet lists 105 'potential stressors' on the left-hand side of the page, with 'A' and 'D' options on the right, relating to strongly agree, agree, neutral, disagree, strongly disagree. The person completing the test circles one letter only. The statements are closely grouped together and the testee must be careful not to leave any out.

Range of applications

Senior management selection, also career development, and dealing with employees suffering from stress who need counselling.

Doing the test

The test, printed on a self-scoring sheet, offers a scale of choices to define the amount of stress exactly, through asking the reader to strongly agree, agree, be neutral, disagree or strongly disagree, according to a list of 105 statements. The statements are simple and straightforward, and it is not difficult to choose between them. Some obviously relate to stressful situations, while others appear to be more general. Overall, the level of face validity is high.

Examples of content of the test

Statements relate to self-perception, need for attention, attitude to independence, the demands of the situation, time stresses, responsibility, performance, money, levels of activity and control, patience and satisfaction with role at work. Typical statements include:

'I don't know what is expected of me'
'I'm too sensitive to the feelings of others'
'I like to have an audience'
'I'm lucky'
'I want my sacrifices to be appreciated'
'The future looks rosy'
'Time works for me, not against me'
'I often try too hard to be successful'
'I sometimes wonder who I really am'
'I worry about what others think'
'I look forward to the unexpected'
'I like to be praised for my achievements'
'I don't like standing in line'
'I have financial difficulties'
'I'm financially secure'
'People accept me the way I am'
'I have trouble relaxing'
'I set new goals before I reach the old'
'I meet my obligations on time'.

Time needed to complete the test

About 10–15 minutes.

Time to score the test

Also about 10–15 minutes, on the self-scoring form which can be carried out by the person administering the test on the spot.

Necessary time for feedback

Could be around 30 minutes or more for a person receiving stress counselling, who is trying to identify and cope with areas of stress in their life. Could be shorter than this when the test is part of a battery of other tests, and nothing unusual is revealed.

Format/structure of the feedback

The stress index is scored according to a grid of levels of high or low stress. Low stress factors are:

self-appreciation;
avoidance of attention;
independence;
desiring demands;
goal comfort;
optimism;
time adequacy;
avoidance of responsibility;
performance comfort;
financial comfort;
being proactive;
having control over life;
being patient;
having job satisfaction; and
having role comfort.

Therefore, a person who is low on stress will be relatively satisfied with themselves overall, will tend to avoid attention, will be independent, will know what they want, will be satisfied with their aims, will be reasonably optimistic, will have time to do what they want to do, will not have huge responsibilities, will be satisfied with their performance generally, will not be worried about money, will be proactive and in charge of their lives, will be fairly patient and, overall, will be satisfied with their role and their vocation.

On the other hand, those who exhibit high stress will be:

self-deprecating;
attention seeking;
approval seeking;
resentful of demands made upon them;
unsure about their goals;
pessimistic;
feeling they do not have enough time;
seeking more responsibility;
anxious about their performance;
worried about money;
reactive rather than proactive;
lacking control over their lives;
impatient;
regretful; and
unhappy with their role at work.

The scores are shown on a chart which is discussed between the person administering the test and the person receiving feedback, with low stress features to the left and high stress features to the right. Those being tested who are low on stress will find that most of their scores are on the left-hand side of the page, and those high on stress will find that their scores mostly occur on the right-hand side. Specific instances of stress experienced by the person undergoing the test can be discussed to substantiate or question the findings.

Value to the employer/user

With the test based upon 105 statements shown at random, it gives an accurate appraisal and a close indication of the perceived stresses of an individual. This instrument is not yet widely used in the UK, although it is valuable in showing how comfortable a person is in their present role and how susceptible they are to stress. It is a very useful instrument in analysing specific areas of stress, and therefore is particularly appropriate in career development exercises. Specific areas of stress can then be addressed, and a strategy for dealing with these and minimising the effects can be evolved. The instrument is also used in the selection process to see how well a person might cope in a potentially stressful job. Thus it is a good choice as part of a battery of tests in a senior management role with a need for clear leadership, without avoidance of responsibility.

Value to the employee/person being tested

As one of the few tests to specifically look at stress indicators, this is a fascinating indication of how stressed or unstressed an individual feels, putting into words what may have been a series of imprecise feelings. It can be comforting to know that the level of stress is generally not high, although there will be areas which need attention. Impatience and time inadequacy can be stressful areas when other stressors are not present. Elements of personal control are either clearly apparent or missing. This is a very revealing short test, adding significantly to findings from other tests, and easy to interpret.

Value to the user organisation

Levels of stress can be clearly linked to corporate cultures. In particular, macho cultures require their people to be able to cope with stress well. They need people who are goal-driven, proactive and in control. Process cultures are more team-oriented and less individualistic, and offer more support to employees. Retail cultures need people who can cope with the work-hard, play-hard demands. High-risk, slow-feedback cultures require goal comfort and patience. This test is a useful adjunct to understanding basic personality types and understanding how they fit into organisations.

Can the test results be deliberately falsified?

It would be possible to appear low stressed, to conceal the amount of stress suffered, but this could then lead to even more stress experienced. If the test is answered as honestly as possible and if areas of stress are revealed, then these can be dealt with in an appropriate way, for the benefit of all concerned.

Advantages over other tests

Looks at stress and how it manifests itself precisely, in much more detail than other tests, and defines areas of stress specifically. It is thus of considerable use in a battery of tests.

Disadvantages compared with other tests

Looks at only one area of personality appraisal, and needs to be combined with other tests for a fuller understanding. American in style, which can be a problem for British readers.

Tests may be combined with . . .

Sweney's Decision Profile, Fleishman's Leadership Opinion Questionnaire, OPQ, Myers Briggs Type Indicator.

Static/predictive value

Provides a useful summary of stresses expressed at the moment when the person is tested, and can help in predicting attitude and reaction to new stresses.

Overall review

Speed of being tested – fast
Speed of scoring results – fast
Cost – low
Range of applications – wide
In-house/Out-house – In-house, under licence
Basic/Advanced – basic

How to prepare yourself for sitting this test

Think of areas where you know you are stressed, and those where you feel quite relaxed. Are you generally quite happy with how you are in your career and your private life? You should complete the test when you are not experiencing extremes, i.e. not unduly stressed and not entirely laid-back.

Will this test produce a different result after a period of time?

It could do, if a person has moved to a much more stressful job, or if they have been made redundant and are facing financial problems. It would be necessary to repeat the test according to each new job situation.

Fleishman's Leadership Opinion Questionnaire

Background

This instrument was developed by Edwin A. Fleishman and copyrighted in 1960 to Science Research Associates Inc., of Chicago, USA (a subsidiary of IBM). The testee is asked to choose the alternative which most closely expresses their opinion of how frequently (as a manager or supervisor) they should do an act as described in each particular statement, so the test is geared towards asking people what they think about specific leadership issues.

The aims of the test

The test aims to analyse the particular leadership style of an individual, especially in terms of how they react towards subordinates, in being directive or delegative.

The format

In 40 questions shown as statements on a self-scoring sheet, the testee is asked about how often a good manager should do a certain thing in a working context, relating to leading and managing a group. The person being tested considers a range of options of how often or seldom they believe that the statement reflects a desirable way to act. The instrument is called a Leadership Opinion Questionnaire, precisely because it is looking at a person's opinions in situations calling for leadership decisions. It is not asking what the person actually does, but what they 'sincerely believe to be the desirable way to act'. The questionnaire introduction specifies that 'different supervisors have different experiences and we are interested only in your opinions'.

Range of applications

For supervisors, managers and executives, in selection, career development and team-building.

Doing the test

The testee is asked to consider the way that a manager should act, expressing their opinions as honestly as possible. There are no right or wrong answers, as such, although clearly, in some cases, doing a managerial job well includes choosing a certain option. Only one alternative can be chosen. The testee is asked to decide between often, fairly often, occasionally, once in a while, and very seldom, for each statement. The testee is again asked to remember that they are considering the statements in a work context, rather than in a leisure or sporting context.

Examples of content of the test

Typical statements within the test include asking how often or seldom the person being tested will:

'refuse to compromise';
'criticise poor work';
'help persons under you with personal problems';
'do personal favours for people under you';
'encourage after-duty work by people in your unit';
'get approval of those under on important matters before you go ahead';
'criticise a specific act rather than an individual';
'insist that everything is done your way';
'treat all people under you as equals';
'reject suggestions for changes';
'talk about how much should be done';
'encourage slow-working people in your unit to work harder'; and
'refuse to explain your actions'.

Time needed to complete the test

The test takes about 10–15 minutes to complete.

Time to score the test

The test is quick to score on a self-scoring sheet.

Necessary time for feedback

About 20 minutes, depending on how satisfactory the results are for the purpose intended.

Format/structure of the feedback

This instrument shows key variables within leadership modes such as the importance of structure to the individual, and whether or not they show sympathy to subordinates. The Fleishman Leadership Opinion Questionnaire can be useful in career development, and the feedback may well be presented in this format.

Should you treat your subordinates with more consideration? Where consideration is low it can be possible to counsel the person on how to accept grievances, and understand their subordinates more effectively.

This instrument also shows the level of task-orientation and the amount of structure and direction needed. As a leader, are you hands-on, or hands-off? Do you let people get on with the job?

Fleishman also gives an indication of leadership style and subordinate style. This instrument is suitable for executives, managers and supervisors, but it is important to norm the results against a relevant group.

Value to the employer/user

The Fleishman instrument can be normed against different groups. This test has been validated against several different cultures and is very successful as a model of leadership. It lists a set of behaviours and the person being tested expresses their opinions against each behaviour pattern. It can thus be useful in selection procedures, in management development and in the creation of teams.

Value to the employee/person being tested

The style of this test, in asking how often these attitudes could be taken, makes the testee think about the topics in a different way.

In this respect, it is quite different from other tests which look at similar topics. In respect to the format of asking questions in this way, there are similarities with the SPQR test. It is particularly useful in showing how much a person needs structure in order to lead successfully, and the extent to which they show consideration to others.

Value to the user organisation

Leadership styles vary a great deal according to the demands of specific organisations. Some styles are successful in macho cultures, and these would include those low on consideration, as these are individualistic working environments. Some cultures would need a more caring and benevolent approach to leadership. The Fleishman exercise is also useful in team-building.

Can the test results be deliberately falsified?

The statements could be answered in a deliberately different way, but this would not help in a selection interview where a particular style of leadership is being sought. It would be impossible suddenly to adopt a different style of leadership according to the demands of a new job.

Advantages over other tests

This test looks in particular at management leadership rather than a range of management skills, in a highly specific way, giving percentile scores which can be compared directly with others in an organisation.

Disadvantages compared with other tests

It is very American in style and very much geared towards those who are supervisors of a unit. It can be used in a senior context and in a non-American setting, but there can be some resistance on account of the style, and the way in which it seems to relate to more junior people. It needs to be combined with other tests to gain a more complete picture.

Tests may be combined with . . .

Can be combined with the Sweney tests, OPQ, Myers Briggs Type Indicator and Thomas-Kilman Modes of Conflict Instrument, and also with Fleishman's own Supervisory Behaviour Description, which allows subordinates to rate their bosses.

The OPQ has a leadership style summary which can be compared with the Fleishman summary; the thinking behind the two is quite different so it is possible to combine the two, especially where leadership is a key issue to be discussed.

Static/predictive value

Can be used to describe current leadership style, especially in terms of being able to operate in certain ways, and predict the way that an individual might behave in a certain group context.

Overall review

Speed of being tested – fast
Speed of scoring results – fast
Cost – low
Range of applications – wide
In-house/Out-house – In-house, under licence
Basic/Advanced – basic

How to prepare yourself for sitting this test

It is useful to think of your style of leadership and how you behave in groups, and how you tend to react to given situations. Think of these situations as you consider the various statements. Be prepared to give instances of why you chose, or why you think you would choose, particular options.

Will this test produce a different result after a period of time?

Possibly, if the individual has been exposed to greater leadership responsibilities in the meantime, and has developed a different attitude towards leadership. It would also need to be repeated after a period of counselling to improve the testee's approach to subordinates.

The Thomas-Kilman Modes of Conflict Instrument

Background

This questionnaire, devised in the USA but used in the UK for selection and career development exercises, dates back to the mid-1970s and stems from Kenneth Thomas's study, *Conflict and Conflict Management*, which was published within a general study of industrial and occupational psychology. This instrument is suited best for the American market for which it was designed, but nevertheless it is highly relevant in any other Western/industrialised corporate context. Few general tests cover this important area of conflict in such detail. It is particularly used by Whitehead Mann Audit & Assessment.

The aims of the test

The Thomas-Kilman Conflict Mode Instrument looks at how a person would respond in debate and discussion, particularly in disagreement. What happens when a person's wishes differ from those of the majority? What are the different strategies for dealing with conflict?

The person being tested is asked to consider how to respond to a conflict situation in which they find themselves and their wishes and attitudes different from those of another person or group of people. The instrument basically looks at sensitivities in dealing with people, and how relationships and information are used.

Thomas-Kilman shows the extent to which a person faces up to conflict. How politically sensitive are they? Do they treat people with diplomacy or lack tact? Do they use bargaining and trading to get things done? Do they keep sight of the larger issues in spite of the outbreak of conflict? How much are they prepared to give in? Do they sometimes appear unreasonable?

The format

The testee is asked to respond to a specific set of 30 statements, listed on a sheet with a) or b) options, and asked to circle a) or b) according to how they would expect to behave, and deciding how characteristic the a)s or b)s are of them.

Range of applications

For general management selection and career development. Also useful for selection of senior candidates for leadership roles.

Doing the test

The test statements are uncomplicated, and it is usually a simple issue to decide which are the most appropriate. The statements do not obviously necessarily relate to conflict situations, but do reveal attitudes. Face validity is fairly high.

Examples of content of the test

(Not possible for copyright reasons.)

Time needed to complete the test

About 10–15 minutes.

Time to score the test

Can be quickly scored on a prepared sheet by the person administering the test, involving adding up scores out of 10 for each of the 5 modes.

Necessary time for feedback

About 20–30 minutes is sufficient.

Format/structure of the feedback

The test, which comprises 30 questions, looks at 5 areas of handling conflict: competing (forcing); collaborating (problem-solving);

compromising (sharing); avoiding (withdrawal); and accommodating (smoothing). How does the person being tested rate themselves according to each method of dealing with conflict?

In scoring, the person doing the test is given a mark out of 10 for each of these attitudes towards conflict. Therefore, the 30 questions actually break down into 6 groups of questions, tackling each different attitude, randomly mixed up in the test.

The scores show how competitive a person is in forcing the discussion towards the desired outcome. They show the following.

1) How collaborative a person is in working with others to achieve a solution to the problem in hand rather than trying to score points off the other people in the team.

2) How much the person is prepared to compromise to get a solution.

3) The extent to which the person is able to share ideas and strategies with others in the interests of accomplishing the tasks.

4) Whether or not the person can implement avoiding tactics, and withdraw from potential conflict. Would the person rather get as far as possible from the dispute and remain outside, even though this means that the opportunity to help make the decision is lost?

5) How accommodating a person is in terms of using the ideas of other people and taking note of their wishes to avoid conflict. Is there a tendency to try to minimise disputes by calming everyone down?

Various academic studies have shown that the five conflict-handling modes are apparent in all conflict situations, defined as incidents when the concerns of at least two people working together appear to be incompatible. In these situations it is possible to describe a person's behaviour in two basic dimensions: first, assertiveness, i.e. the extent to which the individual attempts to satisfy his own concerns and, secondly, co-operativeness, i.e. the extent to which the individual attempts to satisfy the other person's concerns. The five conflict-handling modes can be seen within these two dimensions.

For example, a person who is very competitive is at the top of the assertiveness scale and at the bottom of the co-operativeness scale. A person who is accommodating is at the bottom of the assertiveness scale but at the top of the co-operativeness scale. A collaborating person is at the top of the co-operativeness scale but also at the top of the assertiveness scale. Someone who is avoiding conflict is both unassertive and uncooperative. Compromising is exactly in the middle of all the scales. It is likely that a person will be both competing and collaborative, or avoiding and accom-modating, i.e. they will be either assertive or unassertive. People who are either assertive or unassertive could also be compromis-ing. It is likely that a high score in assertive qualities will be matched by low scores in avoiding and accommodating, and vice versa.

How do we define each of the five types?

A **competitive** person is in a power-oriented mode using whatever power seems appropriate to win, including ability to argue, rank and economic sanctions. Competing can mean stand-ing up for your beliefs or just trying to win, but it is done at the other person's expense.

Accommodating means a person neglecting his or her own con-cerns to satisfy the concerns of the other person or people. Accom-modating involves self-sacrifice, selfless generosity or charity, and yielding to another's point of view even if it clashes with your own.

Avoiding involves the individual not pursuing their own con-cerns or those of anyone else, and refusing to address the conflict at all. Avoiding may mean diplomatically sidestepping an issue, postponing an issue until another time or simply withdrawing from a threatening situation altogether.

Collaborating involves an attempt to work with the other person to find a solution which satisfies both of them. It involves probing an issue to identify the underlying interests of the people in con-flict. Collaborating may take the form of exploring a disagreement from each other's point of view, concluding to resolve some condi-tion which would otherwise have them competing for resources or confronting the difficulties and trying to find a creative solution to an interpersonal problem.

Compromising means finding some expedient and mutually acceptable solution which at least partially satisfies both parties. Compromising gives up more than competing but less than accom-modating. It addresses an issue more directly than avoiding, but does not explore it in the same depth as collaborating. Compromising may mean dividing differences, exchanging concessions or seeking a middle ground position.

All five conflict modes can be useful in certain situations. The effectiveness of a given conflict-handling mode depends upon a specific situation and the way the mode is used. Everyone has an ability to use all five modes, although some predominate because of temperament or practice. How useful is each mode?

The **competing mode** is useful in emergencies and also where unpopular courses of action are needed, such as cost-cutting and discipline. A competing mode can help you to protect yourself against being taken advantage of.

If you scored high in a competing mode you should ask yourself if you are surrounded by yes-men, people who agree with you because they have learned that it is unwise to disagree with you. This can close you off from information. Are subordinates afraid to admit ignorance and uncertainties to you? Are people therefore less able to learn from you?

If you scored low in competition, it could mean that you often feel powerless in situations. It may be that you are unaware of your power or are unable to use it. Do you have trouble taking a firm stand? This may be because you're concerned with others' feelings or the use of power.

A **collaborating mode** is a useful way to find a solution when you cannot compromise between two sets of concerns. Collaborating helps you to learn by testing your own assumptions and understanding the views of others. Collaborating helps in the merging of insights from people with different perspectives, and can help gain commitment through consensus. Collaborating helps to get over problems in interpersonal relationships.

However, people who score high on collaborating should ask themselves if they spend too much time discussing issues in depth which do not deserve such time expenditure. Collaboration takes a good deal of time and energy, and consensus decision-making can sometimes represent a desire to minimise risk, by diffusing responsibility and delaying action. You should also ask yourself whether or not your collaborative behaviour succeeds or fails to elicit collaborative responses from others. In a conflict situation others may disregard collaborative overtures, and the trust and openness which you exhibit in being collaborative may be taken advantage of. You may miss indications of defensiveness, impatience, competitiveness and conflicting interests.

If you scored low on collaborating, you may not be able to see differences as opportunities to learn or solve problems. There are often unproductive aspects of conflict, but indiscriminate pessimism can prevent you from seeing collaborative possibilities, and can deprive you of the satisfaction of achieving a successful collaboration. A person low on collaboration may find that subordinates are uncommitted to their decisions or policies, as perhaps their concerns are not being incorporated.

Compromising mode is useful when goals are moderately important but not worth risking the potential disruption of more assertive modes. Compromising is also useful when two opponents with equal power are strongly committed to mutually exclusive goals. Compromising is also useful in achieving temporary settlements to complex issues, and to arrive at expedient solutions under time pressure. Compromising can be a useful backup mode when collaborating or competing is unsuccessful.

If you scored high in compromising you should ask yourself if you concentrate so heavily upon the practicalities of compromise that you lose sight of the larger issues, such as core values and long-term objectives. Does an emphasis on bargaining and trading create a cynical climate of gamesmanship? Such a climate might undermine interpersonal trust and deflect attention away from the merits of the issues.

If you scored low on compromise you may find yourself too sensitive or embarrassed to be effective in bargaining situations. You may also find it hard to make concessions and, without this safety valve, you may have trouble avoiding mutually destructive arguments and power struggles.

The **avoiding mode** is useful in the case of a trivial or unimportant issue, especially when more important issues are pressing. When you have no chance of affecting the situation the avoiding mode can be most appropriate. When the potential damage of confronting a conflict outweighs the benefits of resolving it, it can be best to avoid it. The avoiding mode is also useful in reducing tensions when people need to cool down, and when it is necessary to gather more information before coming to a decision. The avoiding mode could be used when others can resolve the conflict more effectively and when the issue may indicate another, more basic, issue outside of your responsibility.

If you scored high on avoiding it may be that others will have problems gaining your input. Are you using too much energy avoiding issues rather than facing and resolving them? Are decisions on important issues made by default?

If you scored low on avoiding you may find yourself hurting people's feelings or stirring up hostilities. You may need to exercise more discretion and tact to avoid potentially disrupting a discussion. Do you often feel overwhelmed by too many issues? You may need to devote more time in setting priorities and delegating important issues.

Accommodating is useful when you realise that you are wrong. This allows you a better position to be heard, allows you to learn from others and shows that you are reasonable. Accommodating is appropriate when the issue being discussed is more important to the other person. It then helps in the needs of others and appears as a goodwill gesture, helping to maintain co-operative relationships, which may be useful in the future. Accommodating mode is best when continued competition would damage your cause or when defeat is likely. Accommodating helps to preserve harmony and avoids disruption, and helps subordinates to learn from their own mistakes.

If you are high on accommodating you may feel that your own ideas and concerns are not getting the attention they deserve. Deferring too much to the concerns of others can deprive you of influence, respect and recognition, and minimises your contribution. Those who score high on accommodating may be poor at imposing discipline, and ignoring rules and procedures which are valuable to the organisation.

If you scored low on accommodating, you may have trouble building up goodwill with others. Others may see you as unreasonable and refusing to admit when you are wrong. If you scored low on accommodating, you should ask yourself if you recognise legitimate exceptions to rules, and when to give up.

Value to the employer/user

This instrument is a good discussion tool in analysing how the testee deals with people in a potential conflict situation. Are they good at collaborating? Or do they see everyone as being a competitor? Do they compromise, avoid or accommodate? In a leadership role, it is essential for the attitude to conflict to be clearly understood, within the context of the team for which a person is to be hired, or in which he or she works already.

Value to the employee/person being tested

Thomas-Kilman provides a new way of looking at how conflict is dealt with, and the feedback is invaluable in explaining the positives and negatives of each conflict mode. The testee can be in a better position to analyse when the use of a certain conflict mode is most appropriate, based on the nature of the conflict itself. Everyone has an element of each mode within their characteristics – even if it is comparatively subdued – and can use this to the maximum when required. It helps people to realise that their usual conflict mode is not always suitable, and to learn to be more adaptable.

Value to the user organisation

This instrument is especially valuable in providing a working definition to these attitudes to conflict, which can be very useful in matching a person to a specific corporate culture. Some cultures prefer very competitive people, while others seek those who are more accommodating. The macho culture company would look for people who are in competing mode and, to a certain extent, people who are compromising, in terms of the fact that in macho cultures, there is a need for results oriented people who are dedicated to completing the task in hand. A process culture would prefer people who are accommodating and avoiding. A retail culture would seek competitive people, and a high-risk, low-feedback culture would look for collaborating, combined with accommodating skills.

Can the test results be deliberately falsified?

With difficulty, because of the variety of the statements and the random way in which the different modes are tested. It would also be very inappropriate to attempt to come over as having an unnatural conflict mode, because this could not be sustained in situations of real conflict.

Advantages over other tests

Contains more detail on how conflict is handled than most other tests, and provides a clear way of defining the main attitudes to conflict.

Disadvantages compared with other tests

Looks only at conflict mode and does not consider other aspects of personality, so needs to be accompanied by other tests to reveal further dimensions. Rather American in style and thus may face some user-resistance in the UK.

Tests may be combined with . . .

OPQ, Sweney's Decision Profile, 16-PF, Fleishman's Leadership Opinion Questionnaire, to gain a more complete picture.

Static/predictive value

Good indicator of how a person will behave in a conflict situation, as well as indicating subsidiary conflict modes which can be drawn on when needed.

Overall review

Speed of being tested – fast
Speed of scoring results – fast
Cost – low
Range of applications – wide
In-house/Out-house – In-house, can be licensed-in
Basic/Advanced – Basic

How to prepare yourself for sitting this test

It can be useful to think of the conflict situations you have recently been involved in. How did you react? Do you nearly always react in a certain way, or are you quite adaptable? Do you welcome conflict as a normal part of the working day, or see it as a fairly rare occurrence which you would not greet with much enthusiasm?

Will this test produce a different result after a period of time?

Possibly, but unlikely to be very different, unless the person has experienced a completely contrasting work environment from before, in which conflict is either much more common or much less apparent.

The Insight Profile

Background

Insight was first developed in 1986–7 and was progressively formalised and validated, being launched in mid-1989. The database behind the formulation of Insight has been considerably broadened, especially in reference to other popular psychometric tests which are directly comparable with this particular approach to assessment. Insight has been created and copyrighted by Norman Buckley of Redfield Consulting Limited. Buckley developed Insight as a simpler, more practical and less complex alternative to other main personality tests: he considers that the extra complexity provided by tests going beyond the five basic factors included in Insight does not necessarily add anything to the picture.

Insight was created around the concept that, despite the variety of psychometric models of personality available on the market, they all in fact are based on five main factors of personality. Buckley argues that although the various psychometric tests identified with any particular theory look at personality traits from 2 to 16 (or more) in number, there are in fact 5 main factors which cut through the morass of different traits to reach a workable understanding. Buckley suggests that, although psychologists continue to debate, there is considerable agreement both in the UK and the USA on a general model of five major factors, which do seem to have emerged consistently from the research data, although different theorists tend to apply their own aims and shades of meaning to the traits, as well as different nomenclature.

Insight is based wholly on this distillation of five factors, and the original questionnaire was based on research work undertaken at the University of Edinburgh by Chris Brand.

The aims of the test

Insight has been designed to measure the five personality factors experienced to a greater or lesser degree by all of us. Four of the five factors at the root of Insight – and arguably many other popular tests, according to Buckley – are **will, energy, control and affection**. Underlying these four is the most important factor: **emotionality**. Emotionality is seen as the most significant because it relates to the consistency and predictability of the other factors.

Buckley feels that the consensus among modern personality theorists is that these five factors are required to be represented in any test to cover the range of human individual personality differences. He suggest that only Insight measures these five correctly and concentrates on these exclusively, except for NEO-PI in the US (not included here). Although many of the widely used psychometric tests share a similar structure, they often ignore the concept of emotionality. He believes that an understanding of the big five factors can provide a solid basis for any form of management development programme.

The format

Insight as a test consists of 106 pairs of statements relating to behaviour and attitudes at work. Along a five-point scale, it is necessary to circle a number according to the extent to which you agree with the statement. It is clearly stated that there are no right or wrong answers, just different opinions.

Range of applications

A variety of managerial and professional groups, but used widely in the public sector, especially for selection purposes.

Doing the test

The statements are clear, simple and to the point, and it is generally not difficult to decide upon the extent to which you agree with them or not. They clearly relate to attitudes in the workplace, and mostly are concerned with people-orientation, ability to concentrate, attitude to hierarchies, feelings, arguments and the need to achieve perfection. The face validity of the exercise is high overall.

Examples of content of the test

'In business most people cannot be trusted'	1	2	3	4	5	'In business most people are open and above board'

If the statement on the left is most representative of your views, you should circle the figure **1**. If you feel the statement on the right is most typical, you should circle the figure **5**. Try not to fall back on the middle answer **3**, unless all other answers are completely impossible for you. Other examples of pairs of statements are:

'I'm impatient to get started on new tasks'	1	2	3	4	5	'I can't leave a task till it is finished'

'You've got to look after yourself first : no one else will'	1	2	3	4	5	'We should consider other people's needs first'

'If I have a problem I want to sort it out by myself'	1	2	3	4	5	'When I have a problem I seek the advice of others'

'I would prefer to be known as decisive'	1	2	3	4	5	'I would prefer to be known as supportive'

Time needed to complete the test

About 10–20 minutes.

Time to score the test

About five minutes, including computer-drawn diagram/chart of factor scores.

Necessary time for feedback

About 30–40 minutes, perhaps more if the Insight Profile has been drawn up as a career development exercise.

Format/structure of the feedback

When the test is scored and completed, the person tested is given a booklet introducing the Insight concept, together with the five key personality factors, and also with the four major areas of team focus, interpreted according to the personality indicators. The person is then presented with an individual diagram/chart of a large circle drawn with a square. Within the circle, at 360 degrees, is **will**, at 90 degrees is **control**, at 180 degrees is **affection** and at 270 degrees is **energy**.

In the middle of the circle is a cross in the form of a plus sign, with varying lengths vertically and horizontally, pointing to the four factors to greater or lesser degrees, indicating the importance of **will**, **control**, **affection** and **energy** according to each individual personality. The scores out of 10 for each characteristic are also given, with 1 being the lowest and 10 being the highest. Scores around the 4–7 mark are regarded as average against the norms developed for this test. The **emotionality** scale is also recorded, revealing the all-important feature of whether the person is highly emotional, highly unemotional or average, again according to a mark out of 10.

In the feedback session, the implications of the five factors are explained, starting with the overall impact of emotionality. A very emotional person, subject to dramatic mood swings, will find that their emotionality will affect the dominance of the other characteristics within their personality makeup, whereas a lack of emotionality will undermine the dynamism of these other factors. Degrees of emotionality can affect concentration, confidence, objectivity and perseverance.

The other four factors discussed in the feedback session cover the other personality traits, which Buckley insists are largely the same as those covered in other popular tests, under different names and slightly different interpretations:

will includes independence, self-sufficiency, autonomy, rigidity and decisiveness;

control includes self-control, conscientiousness, conventionality, conformity and conscience:

energy includes extroversion, physical energy, activity, liveliness and involvement;

affection includes sensitivity, trust, helpfulness, openness and compassion.

As a background to these factors, Buckley highlights the importance of emotion and how it can change stability of personality. With a highly emotional person, you cannot be certain that 'What you see is what you get'. With an unemotional person, there is a greater degree of consistency, although with an apparent lack of 'colour' and variety of behaviour. Buckley did not want to emphasise sex differences in his tests, but he did find that women tended to be slightly more emotional than men, according to the findings recorded on his database.

Buckley found that although the emotional factor is not necessarily apparent on meeting a person for a short time, he or she is usually willing to accept it during the feedback session, and to explain their emotions. Buckley finds that most people can accept, if they are very emotional, that they can lose track of priorities and become overwhelmed by their feelings. They can also accept that, if they are not very emotional, they can be seen as boring and lifeless. In the feedback sessions, there has been a general willingness to confirm the test's findings, in Buckley's experience.

The Insight test is also useful in developing leadership profiles, which Buckley defines as four main types: **delegator**, **director**, **coach** and **facilitator**. A control-oriented person is very concerned about career development, and has a need to do better every year, to see clearly that they are progressing. In comparison, a low-control person will 'want it all now'. Control types can delay rewards.

The Insight model defines styles which can be further analysed as follows.

Will has been variously described over the years; researchers have called it dominance, determination, drive and independence. The essence is a strong internal motivation based on firmly-held beliefs. Characteristics are firmness, single-mindedness and goal-directedness. Less favourable qualities are stubbornness and rigidity of view. A common perception is to link drive and determination with aggression, but this need not be the case. Some may use aggression to achieve goals; others may appear submissive and quiet, but be quietly stubborn.

Energy is an element which has, for many years, been identified as extroversion. As the name suggests, it encompasses physical energy, alertness, speed of movement and enthusiasm. Such people are gregarious, competitive, fun-loving, sociable and active. The essence of this dimension is optimism and excitement about doing things. Energy is one of the most visible characteristics and the one which, in Western cultures at least, encompasses many of the most socially desirable traits. Too much energy, however, can lead to over-confidence and over-commitment.

People who score strongly on the **affection** dimension are genuinely positive about other people. They are typically warm and supportive, responsive to others' needs, sympathetic and understanding. They are open-minded and receptive to new ideas and people; they like people and want to be liked. They tend to be selfless (perhaps too much so) and are prepared to sacrifice their own interests for others. They may also be sentimental, and are loyal and trusting, but may be taken advantage of by others who are more cynical.

Control includes self-control, constructive self-criticism and conservatism. Highly-controlled people like order, structure and planning, and prefer to think ahead. Duty and responsibility are cornerstones of control, and high-control people will become frustrated and disillusioned if others don't share their views about right and wrong behaviour. They are conscientious, loyal and ethical, and can be relied upon to apply themselves consistently (even to unpleasant tasks) if they feel it is their duty.

Value to the employer/user

Buckley has applied his Insight theory based on the five factors to look at learning styles, team roles (see below), career choice and leadership theory. Insight has been shown to have considerable value to employers, although it is still relatively under-used in the market and is only recently emerging as an alternative to OPQ, for example.

Value to the employee/person being tested

Insight was used at Ashridge Management College, together with Belbin Team Types, with Belbin providing the team type input and Insight giving a clearer picture of individuals. Insight was seen as very useful in counselling individuals for career development purposes, as well as in selection. Insight has been seen as a way of anticipating and short-circuiting the problems which can emerge for any individual in a job situation.

Value to the user organisation

Insight has been used to build up teams, as an alternative and in conjunction with the Belbin Team Types. It fits in well with the task of selecting people for appropriate corporate cultures. The Insight model looks at teams in terms of the four major areas of focus: **goal-oriented**, **change-oriented**, **people-oriented** and **systems-oriented**. These focuses are derived from the Insight model of individual differences and the differences between these groups are as follows.

1) *Goal-oriented* Teams whose members are primarily goal-oriented will be determined and forceful in trying to achieve end results. They may be seen on the one hand as assertive and committed to the business, but perhaps on the other hand as not always sensitive to the needs and opinions of other people. Similarly, goal-oriented team members will tend to promote the idea that other teams or individuals tend to be much too flexible or easy-going in their attitudes, and by contrast they see themselves as tough and resolute in their determination to achieve.

2) *Change-oriented* Teams whose members are primarily change-oriented will tend to be seen as enthusiastic, energetic, outgoing and hugely optimistic about future potential, and the opportunities which exist. They will tend to engender their own excitement through pursuing 'What if we do this?' type of activities, but of course this may

mean that other people, either within the group or outside it, will feel frustrated by their lack of discipline and lack of structure. Teams like this tend not to want to be constrained and efforts to rein them in may be met with disruption or demotivation.

3) *People-oriented*   Teams whose members are primarily people-oriented will generally be supportive and responsive to other's needs, the sort of group who will listen to each other and be sensitive to opinions which are different from their own. Such teams are generally good at assimilating information and encouraging participation from others. They can, however, also be seen as vacillators or indecisive managers who appear unwilling to commit themselves to a singular course of action, but are always looking for further information.

4) *Systems-oriented*   Teams whose members are primarily systems-oriented will be seen as logical, precise and very structured in their view as to how processes ought to be undertaken. As such, they can be seen as inflexible and pragmatic, but also, perhaps, as lacking the verve and energy of change-oriented teams, lacking the sensitivity and understanding of others as exhibited by people-oriented teams, and as inhibitors of the determinism exhibited by goal-oriented teams. As such, systems-oriented groups are essential and useful within organisations, but they need enhancement from other people with other skill-sets and personality types to be wholly effective.

An Insight analysis of all the members of a team can be seen as valuable in predicting how well the team will work together, and there have been some startlingly successful examples. For instance, a large, well-known retail store chain used Insight in developing teams to run new stores, and an Insight-developed team was brought together in the opening of the new store in a new state-of-the-art shopping centre. This was the first store of the entire chain to hit its targets immediately, despite the fact that it was opened in the middle of a recession. Although other factors were clearly at play here, the use of the Insight test was seen as making a great difference to the working of the team.

Can the test results be deliberately falsified?

Unlikely, because the statements do not obviously relate to the end results. Inconsistencies between test results and the observations of the person administering the test would soon become apparent.

Advantages over other tests

Insight presents simple tools for analysis, and Buckley argues that, by sharing a common language, people being tested can readily understand themselves and their principal personality type. The test results are structured so that people can understand their role within a team and their preferred management style (and even their ability to adapt this style if they wanted to). Insight, Buckley claims, avoids the confusion of multiple models and languages. This fragmentation of psychology into so many models, he argues, can do little to enhance the reputation of psychologists. He may be right, but this does not mean that the existing tests will agree to a common nomenclature. Insight can be used as a viable alternative to many of the other tests on the market, although more work needs to be done on the effect of emotionality on observable behaviour.

Disadvantages compared with other tests

Other tests may provide more detailed appraisal of personality types and more analysis of the implications of these types in an occupational setting. The norm group could be larger (as Insight is yet to be as widely used as some other tests, such as the various OPQ versions) although this is already over 2000.

Tests may be combined with . . .

Buckley has investigated the links between Insight and other well-known psychometric tests. He has categorised the parallel nomenclature relating to his own five factors within the 16 PF, the OPQ and the Myers Briggs, among others. Relating to will, energy, affection, control and emotionality from Insight are, for 16-PF, independence, exvia, pathemia, control and anxiety. The Insight equivalents in OPQ are contesting, extroversion, abstract, methodical and emotionally stable. In Myers Briggs, the equivalents are thinking – feeling, extroversion – introversion, sensing – intuition, and perceiving – judging. Myers Briggs does not measure emotionality. Thus these other tests could be used with Insight to support Insight's findings, and it could also be combined with tests which look at specific areas in more detail, such as decision-making and stress.

Insight has been used as an alternative to the Saville & Holdsworth OPQ, to add to a typical short battery of tests, such as those used by Succession Planning Associates (see under SPQR).

Static/predictive value

Insight presents a good view of the personality of the individual at the moment of testing, and is likely to be useful in predicting behaviour, especially in a team setting.

Overall review

Speed of being tested – fast
Speed of scoring results – fast
Cost – low
Range of applications – general
In-house/Out-house – Out-house, and In-house by trained users
Basic/Advanced – Basic

How to prepare yourself for sitting this test

The test is user-friendly and uncomplicated, and it is only necessary to bear in mind that the answers must relate to an occupational setting. The following feedback session explains the relationship between test answers and test results.

Will this test produce a different result after a period of time?

Possibly, so it is advisable to repeat it after 1 year or 18 months.

The SPQR

Background

This test has been devised by Succession Planning Associates (SPA) as a tool in adding insights about candidates for specific positions in the public sector, especially in local or central government.

A short, simple and specially-designed instrument, it has been used over the last three years as part of a battery of tests given to all candidates considered through this particular executive search consultancy. SPA was founded in 1987–8 by John Smith, formerly head of the public sector search operation of the large diversified consultancy, MSL.

SPQR was developed jointly by SPA and Donald Hudd of Castleton Partners, and was designed as a short and snappy test, specifically for the public sector. It is based on John Smith's experience in public sector search over the last eight years.

The aims of the test

The Succession Planning Questionnaire Response (SPQR) aims to analyse leadership qualities in candidates destined for public sector jobs, and especially considers 12 variables: representation, demand reconciliation, tolerance of uncertainty, persuasiveness, initiating structure, tolerance of freedom, role assumption, consideration, production emphasis, predictive accuracy, integration, and superior orientation (these will be more fully explained later).

These are seen as qualities most appropriate for this particular working environment, and areas which are not adequately explored in other basic personality tests, such as the OPQ.

The format

SPQR takes the form of a list of 100 statements, which must be considered and then personally rated according to individual perception, along a scale of 5 options, choosing from: never, seldom, occasionally, often or always. The statements are listed on the left, the ratings on the right.

The statements are short and simple, and the test has high face validity. It is certainly more straightforward than many other short tests of its type.

Range of applications

Public sector appointments, mostly at senior manager level, and also suitable for CEOs. Could be used outside this sector for any management positions, in theory, but is used exclusively by SPA only.

Doing the test

In each case, one option must be selected. The person being tested is asked not to choose the mid-way, i.e. occasionally, option too often, unless it is absolutely the most appropriate. The statements are less repetitive than similar tests of this type, and presented in clear English.

Examples of content of the test

The questions/statements within SPQR cover a wide range of management topics, as follows.

The leadership of groups and role within groups:

'I act as the spokesperson of the group'
'I make pep talks to stimulate the group'
'I keep the group working together as a team'
'I encourage initiative in the group members'
'I make my attitudes clear to the group'
'I urge the group to beat its previous record'

The questions/statements also look at perceived personal qualities, such as:

'I wait patiently for the results of a decision'
'I am friendly and approachable'
'I keep to myself'
'I can wait just so long, then I blow up'

Many of the questions/statements are about making things happen:

'My arguments are convincing'
'My superiors act favourably on most of my suggestions'
'I handle complex problems efficiently'
'I maintain definite standards of performance'

Some statements may indicate stress, such as:

'I worry about the outcomes of any new procedures'
'I get confused when too many demands are made of me'
'I get swamped by details'
'I get things all tangled up'

Overall, the test has high face validity and is simple and straightforward to complete.

Time to complete the test

About 10 to 15 minutes only. It is not advisable to spend too much time deciding on how often a particular statement applies to you, but instead to answer fairly instinctively.

Time needed to score the test

SPA scores the test from a grid and plots the findings. This is a short task and can be completed on the spot but – as discussed below – results are not given to the candidate until a later stage in the proceedings, so this is not necessary.

Necessary time for feedback

This can range from 20 minutes to about 1 hour. SPA insists that everyone is entitled to personal feedback, even those who do not go forward for the position for which they were a candidate.

Format/structure of the feedback

Feedback is always presented personally and verbally, and SPA do not issue standardised reports, such as the computer-generated OPQ summary. Even feedback by telephone is preferred to a written summary of the findings.

When the test is scored, the qualities of the candidate are analysed in terms of the 12 variables of representation, demand reconciliation, tolerance of uncertainty, persuasiveness, initiating structure, tolerance of freedom, role assumption, consideration, production emphasis, predictive accuracy, integration and superior orientation. Each quality will be discussed in turn between the consultant and the candidate.

Each of these categories is given a score relating to the individual's performance in the test and the preferences which have been chosen. Each category is given a rating which is either low, medium or high. It is possible to see clearly from the results the areas in which the candidate has a low or high propensity. The final figures are totalled in terms of percentiles, and scored against a large norm group, mostly from the public sector. What do these categories actually mean?

The **representation** element is a measure of how well you represent yourself and stand up for yourself, especially in a group situation. Are you often the representative of the group to an outside body? Do you frequently act as the spokesperson of the group?

Demand reconciliation is all about how you cope with the demands of both superiors and subordinates, and how you deal with tasks. How do you reconcile conflicting demands?

Tolerance of uncertainty is clearly concerned with how you perceive what you are doing and where you are going. Are you able to deal with uncertainty or do you respond by building structures to manage it? Do you always try to establish parameters or wait and see what happens?

Persuasiveness is all about convincing others about your ideas and plans. How well do you put across your message? Are you able to get what you want and make sure that others see your point of view?

Initiating structure relates to the setting up of a formalised environment where none exists. Those who do not like uncertainty are likely to be high on creating structures to offset this uncertainty. Do you always prefer order to chaos? Or do you like to encourage free-ranging ideas?

Tolerance of freedom is concerned with the management of subordinates, and also to autonomy and initiative. Do you like things to be clearly laid out or do you prefer more autonomy? How much guidance and direction do you need?

Role assumption is about perception of role and the taking on of other roles. How soon can you fit into a new role? How good are you at playing several roles at once?

Consideration relates to the treatment of others and interest in their views. Do you involve others easily in decision-making and do you take time to consider the interests of others?

Production emphasis is synonymous with task-orientation. How concerned are you with getting the job done? Is this your first priority, over and above taking an interest in the views of others?

Predictive accuracy is all about how well or badly you expect things to turn out and how likely you are to be right about this. Do you also want to keep everything well under control, so it all has a better chance of turning out as you expect?

Integration refers to commitment to the team and developing relationships in the organisation or department. Do you fit in well or do you tend to stay apart?

Superior orientation is about relationships with those in authority. Are you good at working out who is the most powerful person and to whom you should direct your efforts?

The norms used in SPQR have been developed over the last three years from hundreds of people either in the public sector already, or looking to be appointed into it and already seen to be suitable. There tends to be a lack of great swings away from the norm, and comparatively a small variance between people tested, perhaps because most people working in this sector must exhibit a certain degree of collaborative abilities, and are less likely to be strongly individualistic entrepreneurial types, as in the private sector (although this is something of a generalisation).

Value to the employer/user

Roles in local and central government have specific requirements which this test is uniquely prepared to analyse. It has been devised with precise roles in mind, and has been shown to be useful in accurately predicting success in certain roles, working in specific public sector cultures.

Value to the employee/person being tested

As in any other test, SPQR is valuable through providing new insights, and the user-driven nature of the test means that it is clear to see if a person is suitable for a specific role, as well as for the public sector generally.

It can show clearly if the person could make a transition from the private to the public sector. The clear listing of the specific qualities being tested makes this quite a good first test to complete.

Value to the user organisation

The SPQR test has been specifically developed for public sector organisations and the norms also relate to this environment. The results of the test would be quite different if the SPQR test was to be carried out on a varied group of chief executives in the private sector. People in local government mostly relate easily to a process-style culture rather than other corporate cultures, such as the macho and retail styles, and this comes out clearly in the test.

Can the test results be deliberately falsified?

Possibly, but unless this was based on sound inside knowledge of what was required by the particular public sector body, and the culture and style of the group which the person would be working with, there would be little point. And, as John Smith of SPA emphasises, 'it cannot easily be falsified and few have ever attempted it'.

Advantages over other tests

More specifically geared towards the needs of the public sector and quicker to complete than OPQ tests. Has built up more relevant norm groups. Simpler and clearer than many, without Americanisms, which can be confusing to English readers.

Disadvantages compared with other tests

Not as detailed as OPQ, with more limited information in feedback, so not so useful when given on its own.

Tests may be combined with . . .

OPQ 3 and 5 are mostly used, but SPQR could also be combined with PAPI. If the person being tested has never completed a test before, they may be given OPQ 3 in order to familiarise themselves with the process.

Static/predictive value

The SPQR results are recording both static and predictive qualities. Predictively, it is useful in indicating behaviour in groups, and workstyle generally, especially in terms of task and group-orientation.

Overall review

Speed of being tested – fast
Speed of scoring results – fast
Cost – part of SPA service
Range of applications – public sector and others
In-house/Out-house – Out-house at SPA only
Basic/Advanced – basic

How to prepare yourself for sitting this test

It is hardly necessary to consider this, but you must think generally of work experiences rather than social concerns, and answer each statement according to your experience. It can be useful to think up precise instances which match your answers, as these can be valuable in the feedback session, and will help in achieving a better understanding of your work and management style.

Will this test produce a different result after a period of time?

The test results could vary after a person has had different work experiences, and finds themselves in different circumstances, but probably not dramatically. It would need to be repeated after two years or so, but it would be surprising if the results were radically different.

The Omega Motivation and Competency Inventory

Background

The Motivation and Competency Inventory is exclusively offered by Omega Management Consultants, based in St John's Wood in London. Omega have devised this inventory after long experience in developing occupationally-related assessments, and this inventory reflects the current culmination of their work in the field of motivation and competency study. Omega have developed a wide range of behavioural assessments, specialising in preparing comprehensive and behavioural-predicted profiles of executives, which can be matched against specific job requirements. Assessment results can be advised to the individual by written summary, which is usually explained through personal feedback.

Omega offers a series of assessments, of which the Motivation and Competency Inventory is one of the most complex and detailed. Shorter instruments include selected parts of the full Motivation and Competency Inventory, and are offered as alternatives within the Omega 'catalogue' of inventories. Omega's inventories include the Motive Disposition Activity, assessing the individual's motivational drive, taking approximately one hour to complete; the Full Motivation Assessment, taking one to two hours of the individual's time, including job analysis, communication style and managerial style; the Full Motivation and Personality Assessment, taking approximately two hours, which adds 16-PF or Myers Briggs to the above test; the Full Motivation and Competency Inventory, including the major business problem, taking up to six hours, which can additionally include 16-PF, Myers Briggs or CPA. Here, we consider the Motivation and Competency Inventory without these add-ons. The combination of motivation and competency testing, and assessment in this way is unique to Omega.

Omega was established 27 years ago and takes a pride in being very scientifically based, being very concerned about the reliability of their tests and insisting that they must be totally validated before they are used. Their Motivation and Competency Inventory has been developed over a long period: the three motives were identified in the 1940s and the competency bands go back to the early 1970s. The Motivation and Competency Inventory was first developed in its original form in 1972 and has been constantly modified.

The aims of the test

The Motivation and Competency Inventory aims to give the user a good general overview of the individual, as well as a detailed insight into workstyle and approach, based on sound psychological research and a well-developed norm group. The assessment is geared towards analysing general management motivation and competencies, suitable for senior-level management in particular. It aims to be an indispensable tool in senior-level human resource deployment, of long-term value to both the individual and the employer.

The format

The Motivation and Competency Inventory incorporates a number of types of assessment, blended together to form a battery of tests and other instruments, taking about six hours for the individual to complete. There are no time constraints on completing the test, but there are guidelines as to how long each section should take. The motivation section consists of a series of short instruments and a number of pictures about which the person being tested must write stories, followed by the competence section, made up of a longer and highly complex business problem which runs into two distinct parts. The idea is that the person being assessed spends as much time as possible in developing their answers to this key business problem, thereby showing competencies over a broad range of business skill areas.

Range of applications

Generally used in career development exercises and team-building rather than selection, especially by companies who have made a commitment to using this inventory extensively among their fast-track and senior managers.

Doing the test

In doing the test, the person to be tested is given two booklets, one at a time, and must record the answers on the activity form itself, unless otherwise specified (a large pad of lined paper and various coloured pencils are also supplied). The first questionnaire deals with attitudes to intelligence tests. The guidelines make it clear that Omega does not use these types of tests and does not intend to do so. Nevertheless, they consider it worth while to start the battery by asking how the individual feels about these types of tests.

If you have ever taken one of these intelligence tests before, you are asked to remember how you reacted; if you have not, you are asked to imagine how you would expect to react. In this questionnaire, it is necessary to put a cross on a point along a grid line, with the mid-point indicated for guidance only. This system of indication allows for the accurate expression of strength of feeling or attitude about the particular question. Omega ask the person being tested to be as frank and as honest as possible. The questions relate to emotional feelings during an intelligence test, the degree of confidence or anxiety and extent to which the individual may avoid having to take the test in the first place. There are 12 questions only.

Then the motivational survey proper begins, seen as a fun questionnaire with a serious purpose, designed to discover an individual's own perception of their inner drives and temperaments, being asked to place a cross next to the option which is seen as most appropriate. Each question has 3 options and there are 40 questions. These first 40 questions are certainly interesting and amusing, and should cause few problems in making a choice between the options.

The third section, 'Motive disposition activity', asks the person being assessed to consider a series of six pictures and write out brief, imaginative stories about each. These stories should take between 5 and 10 minutes to complete and should discuss what is happening in the pictures, who the people are, what led up to the situation, what they are thinking about, what they want, what will happen and what will be done. However, the stories should not be just a series of answers to these questions, but continuous flowing narrative. The individual is asked to make the stories interesting and dramatic, to show an understanding of people, and concern and involvement in human situations. The six pictures are variable in style, some including a good deal of detail, and others relatively little. This task could prove difficult for those unused to descriptive or imaginative writing, especially because six stories can be quite difficult to write in rapid succession with only short gaps for thought in between, although Omega receive very few complaints that the six stories are difficult to write.

The fourth section is labelled 'Work analysis questionnaire' and is designed to discover the kind of work the individual is involved in, in terms of the demands and pressures, and how these affect job performance and satisfaction. This questionnaire needs to reflect an accurate description of the individual's work and feelings about it. The person completing the test is asked to consider each of 37 question, marking a cross within a sliding scale which offers 5 choices between negative and positive. The negative end of the scale reflects a point which is least characteristic of the job in discussion, with the positive end as the most characteristic. These questions ask about aspects of the individual's job in a simple statement, which will be seen as either negative or positive.

The fifth element within the Inventory is the 'Communication style questionnaire'. This invites the individual to think about their attitude to the job in relation to the handling of colleagues and subordinates. There are 40 pairs of statements which may describe some aspects of the job in terms of communications. The individual should read each pair of statements and decide which one best applies, then circle either a) or b). If the person has no colleagues or subordinates, they should just imagine how they would handle them and answer the questions accordingly. Sometimes it is difficult to distinguish between the statements, as both or neither seem to apply, but it is necessary to make a choice. A number of the statements are repeated throughout the test against other statements, so there appears to be an element of repetition, which can occasionally be irksome.

The sixth part of the Motivation and Competence Inventory is the 'Managerial style questionnaire', designed to help in the

understanding of the kind of managerial style which is characteristic of the individual. The questionnaire consists of 20 statements,
again to be answered by a cross along a scale from negative to
positive. Not all of the statements will be relevant to the job in
question, but it is important to make a judgement in each instance.
Frankness and honesty are essential to provide an accurate insight
into managerial style. The statements express beliefs and attitudes
about work environments, the nature of projects, relationships,
standards, rewards and controls. This is straightforward and
relatively easy to make a decision upon in each case.

At this point, the short instruments within the Motivation and
Competency Inventory come to an end and the major business
problem begins. This problem, in two parts, involves a careful
evaluation of the data supplied, and the formulation of a number
of decisions, both strategic and tactical. Different decisions are
possible and reasonable, there are no right or wrong answers, and
the most important point is that the reasons for each decision
should be clearly explained and convincingly argued. The two
parts of the problem are distinct and should be answered in turn,
separately. The first part is expected to take about two hours, the
second part less than an hour.

The problem answers must be written out on a separate pad,
using simple aids – coloured pencils, a ruler, a calculator etc. – and
ideally in as much detail and depth as possible. The problem is
extensive, involving role-playing, writing business and marketing
plans, and financial feasibility studies. Rapid decision-making
based on sparse data is necessary. The handling and instructing of
subordinates is needed, together with interpreting their findings
and digesting their advice. Choices must be made and justified in
the context of the desired objectives of the business plan. The
problem calls for a degree of financial planning skills, marketing
and PR ideas, analysis of commercial potential and general business common sense. The problem tests report-writing ability,
width of commercial vision, understanding of the initial objectives
and translating them into action, and sustaining an idea through a
number of stages towards a viable venture.

The second part of the problem looks at the original venture
further down the line, when it requires immediate follow-up
action. This requires an imaginative response to difficult scenarios,
and an ability to motivate and convince subordinates in times of
difficulty. It calls for the ability to digest more data which alters the

original picture, and act upon this accordingly. It reveals either an optimistic or pessimistic attitude to a problem, and the level of commitment to see a venture through to its completion.

Examples of content of the test

Of the first main questionnaire, comprising 40 questions, there is a need for some imagination, such as:

'If I were stranded on a desert island, I would . . .
a) read *Ice Station Zebra* while waiting to be rescued,
b) read *Flora and Fauna of Antarctica* while waiting to be rescued, or
c) forget about reading and swim for the mainland.'

Other statements are more immediately job-related, such as:

'In my work I prefer to:
a) carry out a project myself,
b) manage a group of people, or
c) co-ordinate different groups of people.'

There are two questions asking which word appeals to you most. One offers a choice between 'a) improve, b) participate, and c) help', clearly work-related concepts; the second group of words is 'a) raunchy, b) production, and c) neighbour'.

Other questions include, 'I get more "kick" in my work from a) networking, b) convincing my boss to accept my ideas, or c) satisfying myself that I have found the best solution to a tricky problem'.

Of the six pictures in the third section about which you must write stories, some include two people, one person or a group of people, leaving plenty of scope for interpretation. They are drawn in different styles, some clearly and precisely, others more impressionistically. Some are obviously work-related, others not necessarily so.

Typical statements in the fourth section, relating to aspects of the job of the person being tested, include:

'feedback on goal achievement in my job is available in a measurable way';

'in this job the results mostly depend upon the results of my subordinates';
'my job requires me to work alone most of the time'.

The statements discuss whether or not the job is challenging, sociable, goal-oriented, controlled and the way in which most of the time is spent.

Examples of the pairs of statements in the fifth section, relating to communication style, include:

'a) I believe that once targets have been agreed, my team members should be self-motivated enough to reach them, and b) I believe that a popular leader is better than an unpopular one';

'a) I think team members should use their own abilities and resources to find solutions for difficult tasks, and b) When a subordinate disagrees with me, I take care to explain why I want something done in a certain way'.

Typical statements of the sixth section, relating to managerial style, include:

'I expect people to check with me before making decisions';
'At least once a week I single out someone doing a good job and commend them personally';
'I like to be sure that all assignments are clearly-defined and logically structured'.

Time needed to complete the test

Six hours. A typical format is to start at 9.30 a.m. or 10 a.m., break for lunch and continue until 4.30 p.m. or 5 p.m.

Time to score the test

Also a number of hours, according to a precise scoring format which has been developed by Omega. It is not possible to do the test and receive the feedback on the same occasion.

Necessary time for feedback

At least two hours, in which to explain the background to the tests and the psychological research on which they are based, and the nature of the findings. The person being tested can return again to Omega for further feedback once they have had an opportunity to digest these findings.

Format/structure of the feedback

The person being tested is presented with a lengthy folder introducing the findings in detail, and showing individual results. Dr George New, the founder of Omega, often conducts the feedback session of the Motivation and Competency Inventory personally. This will be accompanied by the issuing of this large document, including five chapters of information, of about 50+ pages in length. The feedback is based on this results booklet, and there is a need to explain a number of specially drawn charts within this, which show each person's individual results. It is often seen as necessary to have a second feedback session in which subsequent questions can be discussed. The test breaks down to up to 200 different individual characteristics, which is rather a lot to digest in one meeting, especially for someone new to this, more advanced, form of psychological testing. These results can be confusing and the scoring mechanism is clearly very complex. The questioning of results subsequently is greatly encouraged, so this feedback is seen very much as an interactive process.

In looking at motivation, the test analyses managerial philosophy, producing a pragmatic, broad-brush insight, rather than looking at details. This is based on what Dr New sees as a 'sampling of the mind'. This exercise refers back to the six pictures, which are described by the person doing the test in the early part of the exercise. These are six fixed stimuli which provoke thoughts and reactions, which can be analysed by a psychologist. Dr New likens this to taking a blood sample: the blood taken from any part of the body is reckoned to be the same as from any other part. Similarly, this sample of the mind is supposed to be representative of the whole.

The basis of the motivation assessment is the theory that there is a correlation between the way people behave and what is in their minds, or what they are thinking about most of the time. Behind this theory is an empirical study, carried out on a very large group of people, analysing thought patterns. There are, apparently, three broad bands of thinking present in every person, which characterise their behaviour, and define basic motives which predict behaviour. The three basic motivations (called **primary social motivations**) are:

need for **achievement**;

need for **affiliation**; and

need for **power**.

In terms of the choice of words used to describe them, these are now seen as rather approximate descriptions and it is possible that the three basic motivations may be renamed in the future.

The purpose of the motivation aspect of the test is to measure the frequency of these motivations in the individual's thought patterns. These are based on North-West European norms, both male and female, of a population of over 5,000. The norm is not skewed to any one profession and covers a range of occupations, including students and blue-collar workers. The whole idea is to develop a profile to map the mind.

The format of the stories, and the literary style used, are not important in the scoring, but the content is. The stories reflect the mind and its workings, and are arguably truly reflective of these unless they are written under the influence of trauma, alcohol or drugs. The request to write the stories is presented to the person doing the test at least 20 minutes into the exercise, so that the person being assessed is fully relaxed by this stage. The earlier tests in the assessment are mostly intended to set the scene. The pictures act as an external stimulus to attract responses, and this is one of the most revealing aspects of the test. When we know what our motivations are, we will know how we will behave in a given situation. As most people exhibit a combination of motivations, there could be an element of each present, but in most cases, one motivation will predominate. The knowledge of the mind obtained from this test can help predict how the individual will behave.

Each person's motivations are established at around the time of puberty, and the chance of changing them afterwards is low. But even if motives cannot be changed, situations can be changed and, therefore, knowing a person's motivations can be very important in putting them into situations in which they can be most effective. Clearly, the right situation can improve motivation.

The three basic motives predict about 80 per cent of an individual's behaviour, but as we have said, one will usually predominate as a result of a situational trigger. What are the characteristics of these three motivations?

Achievement-motivation is very task-related, and is characteristic of people who want to do things by themselves, who want feedback and want to know results. This motivation characterises people who are good at selling, are entrepreneurial, and who need a constant and/or moderate risk challenge. There is not so much of an element of control here and there is not much sensitivity to relationships.

The **affiliation-motivation** type is the most sensitive to other people and is typical of those who can't cope alone, and who are so close to people that they almost know what they are thinking before they speak. They like non-threatening behaviour and are not task-motivated. Many very affiliative people have problems making a success in the commercial world.

Power-motivated people need to make an impact, to feel influential, to be assertive. This motivation is more complex than the other two, with four different stages of power (see below).

Seventy per cent of people have one dominant motive of these three, and having two strong ones can be difficult, in terms of confusing the picture of predictive behaviour. Relatively few people have all three motivations, and they can act in a quite unpredictable way.

The power-motivation is expressed in four stages, which can change during the life of an individual. People influenced by the power-motivation can progress from stage 1 to stage 4, although they cannot regress. The first stage of power is **dependent power**, in which power is obtained through another person or through a symbol of power, such as a uniform. People with predominant stage 1 power can be loyal, helpful and dedicated.

Second stage power is **independent power**, in which the person wants to do everything their own way, exhibiting control over themselves and their surroundings. They can be rebellious, argumentative and hard to manage, yet are tidy and organised, and systematic in approach.

Third stage power is the **empowering of others**, seen through the transmitting of power to others, which is an influencing, guiding and helping form of power. Third stage power can be divided between personal assertive power and social assertive power. The latter can be an essential leadership quality in a person, as a characteristic of this second aspect of third stage power is an appeal to carry out a task for the good of everyone.

Fourth stage power is the most sophisticated and is fairly unusual, representing the individual as **a conduit of power**. They have no personal power, but exude power bestowed upon them from outside; almost a religious form of power.

Those who are influenced by power-motivation usually have more than one form present, although usually one stage predominates at any given time.

The feedback then includes a useful insight into assessing the match between your motives and your job. Your motivation profile, established above, is matched to your perception of your job. Do the demands of your job have a similar profile in need for achievement, need for affiliation and need for power? A close match between your personal motives profile and your perceived job needs profile will mean maximum motivation in your work. If there are significant discrepancies, this can lead to frustration, unhappiness and demotivation. As the feedback document points out, 'there are no right or wrong motivating drives. What is important is that we find the appropriate situations in life to fulfil our needs.' To validate your job profile, you must answer the following questions:

How do you spend your time – what do you actually do at work?

Which of these activities do you find easy, fun and enjoyable, as opposed to frustrating, or a hassle?

What kind of positive and negative feedback do you receive?

Who among your peers is doing particularly well in a job similar to yours?

How do you see your job changing in the future?

What would the motive requirements of your ideal job be?

If your personal motive profile is higher than your job motive requirement, you may experience frustration. If the reverse is true, you may feel anxiety. If the shape of the profiles is the same but the job profile is lower, this can lead to boredom; the other way round, and you could feel exhaustion. The ideal is that the profiles are of the same shape, with the job motive about 25 per cent higher, so 'that there is a degree of challenge in the job and you feel comfortably stretched'.

The primary social motivations profile drives everything else in the feedback, and is largely revealed by the way you have written the six stories. After establishing these primary social motivations, the feedback moves to an analysis of **initiative and response**: in your behaviour do you generate new situations or respond to existing situations? There are five parameters shown by the initiative response indicator: the need to **visualise**, **generate**, **philosophise**, **reflect** and **evaluate**. The first two are proactive, whereas the second three are more reactive. In most corporate settings, there is a greater need to be responsive than to show initiative. Someone with a very high initiative would be very frustrated if they could not express this, and would be happier in a research setting, perhaps in a university, or working for themselves or in a very small organisation.

The analysis of initiative and response is followed by feedback on **communication style:** as the feedback booklet explains:

Communication style is the way we talk to other people in a work situation and is a learnt management technique which you either acquire through pressure of the environment or by deliberate learning. It is important to distinguish between 'motives' and 'communication style'. We have already discussed that 'motive' is a pattern of thought, and in our assessment we concentrate on the three primary social motives [PSMs] which control the majority of our behaviour. Motives are in our mind and are not visible. They become visible when a situation arouses the motive required, and we start behaving in a certain way depending on our PSM make up. This can be represented in the simple equation:

$$\text{BEHAVIOUR} = \text{MOTIVES} \times \text{SITUATION}$$

Communication style is one of the major elements to affect the situation, i.e. the style or styles that you as a manager use will arouse one of the three PSMs in the person to whom you are talking.

Communication style defines how you talk to and interact with your colleagues and staff and is measured by the following six styles:

pace setter
coach
affiliator
democrat
coercer
authoritarian

Two of the above styles will arouse one of the three primary social motives in the person, or group of people, with whom you are communicating. Thus:

pace setter and coach	AROUSE	achievement motivation
affiliator and democrat	AROUSE	affiliation motivation
coercer and authoritarian	AROUSE	power motivation

A point to remember as you examine your profile is that there is no single successful communication style. The success of any individual style is determined by the needs of your staff and the objective demands of the situation. There is NO correlation between your PSM profile and your communication style.

For example, if you are a sales manager, your success would be related to the high achievement motivation of your sales people. You, as a manager, would want to arouse and reinforce achievement motivated behaviour in your team. You would use the coach communication style, i.e. you will give them performance feedback on a regular basis, and ensure that sales goals are clearly identified and are challenging, but achievable. You would be concerned with the final outcome, but would not attempt to control how your sales people did their jobs. It is likely that the performance of your staff would be poor if you attempted, in 'this situation', to manage in a coercer style.

There are some situations, however, where a directive style of communication may be appropriate and in this case you may want to use the authoritarian or even coercer style. If the situation requires the consent of a group of people, the democrat style would be the most effective.

To summarise, the six styles are: **pace setter**, **coach**, **affiliator**, **democrat**, **coercer and authoritarian**. Pace setter and coach arouse achiever-motivation; affiliator and democrat arouse affiliation-motivation; and coercer and authoritarian arouse power-motivation. Most people have a dominant style and perhaps a secondary style, and would alternate between these, depending on the situation. Some people also have a backup style, which they may use if their dominant style is not effective. All these styles can be effective in their own way, but the coach, democrat and authoritarian styles are most effective in general managerial behaviour.

After considering communication style, the Omega assessment then looks at **managerial style**. What kind of work climate would you generate? This is not necessarily how you behave now, but a statement of intent. There are five parameters in the managerial style profile: **conformity**, **responsibility**, **standards**, **rewards**, and **warmth and support**. Ideally, in a management context, conformity should be low, as too many rules would restrict initiative from subordinates. This is a profile of the working climate of your team, and you must consider this when employing people to work with you. This is your perception of what you might do, but it is not necessarily what you would do in practice. If there is a discrepancy between your managerial style profile and the organisational climate which you think you should create, then there may be scope for questioning your apparent profile. By contrast to low conformity, other styles include high responsibility, standards, rewards, warmth and support.

The assessment then moves on towards analysing **general management competencies**. How do you perform your management responsibilities? There is a need to know about your job in detail to get a useful result here. Within this particular exercise, it is not possible to analyse job specific competencies or corporate specific competencies, so concentration is on general management competencies. This assessment is based on the response to the solving of the major business problem, which reflects your approach to work and your competencies. The relative strengths within your management competency profile therefore requires analysis and interpretation in relation to the demands of the job. The evaluation is made according to the experience of the individual undertaking the test, whether they be a graduate recruit or the chief executive of a large multinational.

This major business problem analyses 30 individual competencies, and these are categorised into 8 underlying management competency bands. Thus, you are assessed against your peers in a closely defined way. The eight competency bands are:

action management;
change management;
co-ordination;
creativity;
leadership;
motivation;
organisation; and
planning.

These competencies can be encouraged and developed by the individual if there is a perceived need, but this can take a major commitment.

The assessment then considers the interaction between general management competencies and the three primary social motives. It is recommended that you should look at your strengths and how these can be developed, as well as being conscious of weaknesses, although it is better to concentrate on strengths. The assessment would enable you to team up with someone who has strengths where you are seen to have weaknesses. This analysis is thus particularly useful in team-building and career development exercises.

The interaction between general management competencies and motivations can show synergies, or lack of them, with the ideal of achieving harmony between your competency and your motives. A detailed chart is produced at the end of the feedback document, analysing the incidence of the different bands with an analysis of how these fit in with your motivation pattern. This all goes back to original thought patterns, which are revealed in your approach to the major business problem within the test.

Value to the employer/user

The Motivation and Competency Inventory (latest version devised in May 1991) is seen by many users as a practical, powerful and accurate way of measuring characteristics which assess the way an individual is likely to perform in, or adapt to, various types and levels of managerial jobs. The Inventory aims to identify key areas of weakness or strength, and provides specific actionable guidelines on staff development, recruitment, career planning and organisation change. Different formats of the test are available for specific jobs and specific company cultures. In some cases, Omega devises structured questionnaires for whole teams of people within a particular company.

Omega claim a unique view of the analysis of motives, but accept that the process takes much longer than so-called superficial tests, and the employers using the test need to know a lot about it too. Thus, they tend to have a relatively small client base, but the clients are very long term, and have built many of their teams through using Omega tests.

Value to the employee/person being tested

Omega claim that no one else in the psychological testing market place offers such in-depth insight into the working of people's minds, in such an occupationally-oriented way. They suggest that people who have been tested by them should keep their feedback results with them and use this as a blueprint in the development of their careers. This inventory certainly presents a new way of analysing motivation, and is particularly valuable in explaining how you feel about your job.

Value to the user organisation

Until the late 1970s, the market in the UK was generally unreceptive to testing, but some of Omega's clients date back to that point, and have followed the techniques loyally. Omega prefer most of all to offer a continual process of analysis to specific teams of people in an organisation. Each client also receives an executive summary, indicating how the person should best be deployed in the organisation, and Omega is able to make recommendations on individuals for training purposes. By comparison, Dr New argues, other tests are not able to penetrate the mind, and therefore the feedback is correspondingly less valuable. Many of the user organisations are large, blue-chip companies, often with process cultures.

Can the test results be deliberately falsified?

No, because the format of the test is such that you are revealing details of your psyche without knowing exactly what the testers are looking for. The way you write the stories and the angle you take, and the way you prepare the business plan, could not be altered to present anything other than what you are.

Advantages over other tests

The Motivation and Competency Inventory provides deep psychological insights, and is arguably more occupationally-oriented than the DMT. It provides a very full and detailed picture of the individual at work, more so than the OPQ or any of the other, shorter tests, and cannot be falsified.

Disadvantages compared with other tests

This test is very time-consuming and expensive, and the feedback can be complex and difficult to understand for someone not experienced in psychology.

Tests may be combined with . . .

This test is combined, in its extended version, with Myers Briggs or 16-PF. It could also be compared with the insights given by the DMT, for a very full psychological insight.

Static/predictive value

Provides useful and detailed analysis of how a person behaves in their job, and how they feel about it, and can predict how they would behave in a given job situation, and can suggest how the job situation could be changed to increase motivation.

Overall review

Speed of being tested – slow
Speed of scoring results – slow, but within 36 hours if required
Cost – high
Range of applications – career development of senior executives

In-house/Out-house – Out-house at Omega, or Omega can visit
  the client
Basic/Advanced – advanced

How to prepare yourself for sitting this test

This is a long one, so you must leave the day free and not worry
about what is happening back at the office. You must be prepared
to concentrate hard, especially on the pictures and the business
problem, and work systematically and carefully, pretending that it
is a 'real' task, which needs your best ideas and insight.

Will this test produce a different result after a period of time?

Possibly, as a person gains in experience with dealing with precise
business situations, but it would be necessary to tackle a different
business problem, because it would be likely that the person would
remember how they answered the first time. As discussed under
feedback, the stage of power of a power-motivated individual can
change during their life.

Raven's Progressive Matrices

Background

This is an abstract reasoning test, rather like the GMA version, but is more traditional and old established, and more extensive norm groups have been developed. Norms for Raven's Matrices have now been developed in many countries of the world, and some for specific age, ethnic and occupational groups. It can be used widely as an ability and intelligence test but it is included here because of its increasingly common use in the testing of strategic thinking among senior executives. For example, this interpretation of its use is practised by Pintab Associates.

When John Raven (a psychologist based in Edinburgh) devised the tests, he was convinced that better results were obtained when it was untimed, but there has been wide demand for their use in group settings where convenience dictates that everyone should finish the test together. When the test is timed, it should be normed against timed norms. The tests have been developed over more than 30 years, with the initial series first published in 1938 and the second series in 1947. Each series has been revised in the light of more research.

Raven's Progressive Matrices have been devised to be used with other tests, especially with tests of verbal and numerical reasoning, but they are included in this book among a series of personality tests because of the insight they provide into strategic thinking.

The aims of the test

Raven's Progressive Matrices are very well-known ability tests, which can also be used to reveal a great deal about thinking conceptually and autonomously. They question strategic capacity, and the ability to stand back and look at a problem from a distance. In many cases, psychologists use Raven's as an intelligence test, but others use it as an approach to problem-solving, especially when the person is asked to explain why they made a certain choice. Senior executive selection processes are including Raven's when there is a need for a visionary approach.

The format

Raven's Progressive Matrices consist of 36 puzzles. Each puzzle has three rows of three designs, with a final one missing. It is necessary to use increasing intellectual judgement to decide which is the continuing image to fill in the gap, based on what has gone before, and a series of options are given below the design to be completed, from which to choose. The puzzles are all visual images, based on different shapes and forms, both complete and incomplete, in outline form and solid.

Range of applications

As an intelligence test for general use, or specifically in senior executive selection to test strategic and conceptual thinking patterns.

Doing the test

This test requires a good sense of logic and strategic thinking for a high score. Many accountants, engineers and also senior executives in strategic planning roles enjoy doing these tests and gain high marks.

Raven's Matrices can be used at the outset to analyse the basic intelligence of the person being tested, and this is done in the process of explaining how the test should be approached, when the person doing the test sits down in front of the question manual. Within the first few minutes it is clear whether or not the person being tested comes with the 'dullest' 10 per cent of adults, the 'average' 80 per cent, or the 'brightest' 10 per cent. This is ascertained from doing the first problem of the set, which takes only a few moments. If a person makes a mistake at any stage of the initial test they are warned that they should look closely at the pattern to remember that one – and only one – of the eight pieces shown is right, and to be sure that a choice is made of the one which makes the pattern correct both along and down the scales. This exercise is useful in giving the person doing the test some confidence that they know what they are doing.

In doing this test at Pintab, one of the problems within the series of 36 is seen as particularly revealing, and the person administering the test will question the person completing the test as to the logic behind the decision they made. They are asked to reason through their selection of the answer to this specific problem and this reveals not only the logic they used to answer the problem but some degree of the confidence they have in their judgement.

Some people, especially those who are very competitive, will argue against the tester even when they are told they are wrong. The way in which the problem is approached often shows that someone may be on the right track at the beginning of the test or situation but fail to follow through.

Some people are put off when the tester takes a great interest in what they are doing and wanders around the room occasionally looking over their shoulders, while others use it to make themselves try harder. Completing the Raven's test requires an entirely different kind of thinking, which may or may not be affected by interruptions. Pintab occasionally used this technique to check intellectual confidence, but normally it is administered without anyone standing over you or walking around!

Doing abstract problems means that each problem must be solved separately, and after it has been completed, then the thinking behind that solution should be jettisoned, and each problem looked at freshly. This is in considerable contrast with the Watson Glaser Test, which requires sustained concentration.

When working at speed some people attempt a large number of problems, and guess at the answers when they do not clearly see the solution. Others prefer to tackle fewer problems, but make fewer mistakes, making certain that they have solved each problem correctly before going on to the next. In either case, the output of efficient intellectual activity appears to be almost the same, according to studies of Raven's results over the years. The main difference is that the former uses up more of the test material in 40 minutes, and cannot greatly increase the score when people are allowed to go on working until they have finished. The maximum output of efficient intellectual work involves using both material and time well.

Examples of content of the test

(Not possible for copyright reasons.)

Time needed to complete the test

Forty minutes, strictly timed.

Time to score the test

Quick, based on self-scoring answer sheets, so that feedback can be given in the same session.

Necessary time for feedback

About 20–30 minutes, depending on the use of the test.

Format/structure of the feedback

The person giving feedback will explain that, according to the official manual accompanying the Advanced Progressive Matrices, they can be used to discriminate between people of superior intellectual ability in one of two ways:

- without a time limit, they can be used to assess observation and clarity of thinking;
- with a time limit, usually of 40 minutes, they can be used to assess intellectual efficiency.

At the first attempt, it is unlikely that anyone of even outstanding intellectual capacity can solve the problems in less than 40 minutes, while it is possible for someone to work on them for well over an hour without becoming bored.

In feedback, there will also be an opportunity to discuss common errors in completing the Matrices, which have been identified by psychologists over the years as:

incomplete solutions;
arbitrary lines of reasoning;
overdetermined choices; and
repetitions.

'Incomplete solutions' are due to people failing to grasp all the variables determining the nature of the correct figure required to complete a problem. Instead, they chose a figure which was right as far as it went but was only partly correct, and an essential element was still missing.

'Arbitrary lines of reasoning' was the reason for the error when the figure chosen suggests that the person has used a principle of reasoning qualitatively different from that demanded by the problem. They thought about the problem in a totally different way and so missed the correct answer completely.

'Overdetermined choices' are mistakes involving a failure to discriminate between irrelevant qualities in the figure chosen and when the person being tested chooses a figure which combines as many as possible of the individual characters shown within the matrix to be completed. It seems quite an easy option, which looks most likely to be correct, without determining why exactly. This may be regarded as a form of overinclusive thinking.

(Psychologists have found that many people who are schizophrenic answer in this way, but as people who are certainly not schizophrenic make errors of this type as well, they describe this form of error as a 'confluence of ideas' rather than suggesting that there is a deeper meaning involved.)

'Repetitions' are mistakes made by people who simply selected a figure identical with one of three figures in the matrix immediately next to the space to be filled, which defeats the objects of the test and shows a failure to grasp the object of the test.

The amount of the test completed in 40 minutes, when the person doing the test did not know they would be allowed extra time, naturally affects the number left over later. So, the total scores from unlimited time are not identical with the scores which might have been obtained if people were allowed to complete the problems as an untimed test. People who, in 40 minutes, attempted all but the last 4 problems in the scale were severely handicapped. In other words, people tend to differ more in their rate of work than in their intellectual capacity.

Value to the employer/user

Each problem within Raven's Matrices has been devised as a system of thought, while the order in which the problems are presented provides the standard training in the method of working. This explains the expression 'Progressive Matrices'. In this respect, they are invaluable in analysing thinking patterns and the ability of people to grasp complex thought processes. By themselves, they are not tests of general intelligence, and it is always a mistake to describe them as such.

Raven's Matrices are also useful in understanding a person's speed of accurate intellectual work, as distinct from capacity for orderly thinking. Because the tests include simple problems which grow more difficult, a person's speed of intellectual work cannot be deduced from the number of problems solved in a fixed time. It is not necessary for everyone to attempt every problem before stopping. By imposing a time limit, a person's intellectual efficiency, in the sense of speed of accurate intellectual work, can be assessed. This is generally, but not always, related to capacity for orderly thinking. A knowledge of a person's intellectual efficiency is useful in assessing their suitability for work which requires quick, accurate judgements.

Value to the employee/person being tested

Raven's Progressive Matrices can provide the person doing the test with new insight into their way of thinking. It can be quite sobering to realise that, according to research on Raven's results, based on people having completed the matrices over a number of years, the capacity to form comparisons and reason by analogy increases rapidly during childhood, and appears to have reached its maximum around the age of $14\frac{1}{2}$. This ability stays relatively constant for about 10 years, and then begins to decline, slowly but with an apparently remarkable uniformity right through to old age. So it can be difficult to improve performance radically in completing the Matrices successfully by taking them again at a later date.

It has been suggested that, by the age of about 14, a child's trainability has reached its maximum, while after the age of 30, a person's ability to understand a new method of thinking and adopt new methods of working, and even to adjust to a new environment, steadily decreases.

The decline continues at the same rate after the age of 60. By the age of 80, a person's score on the Matrices would probably be less than that of a child of only 8.

Value to the user organisation

The Matrices can help in matching people to cultures where a good deal of strategic thinking is needed, such as the high-risk, slow-feedback cultures and, to a certain extent, in companies with a macho culture. The Matrices can also be valuable in the formation of teams. The same comments relating to the use of GMA Abstract Tests also apply here.

Can the test results be deliberately falsified?

Only by practising with the Matrices and perhaps learning the results off by heart, but the people administering the tests are on the look-out for this.

Advantages over other tests

The Matrices provide a very useful insight into conceptual thinking, especially when normed against a senior executive group.

Disadvantages compared with other tests

The Matrices need to be combined with other tests to give a further dimension. They are quite taxing and give the impression of being sent back to school. They don't appear to have high face validity for senior executive roles, and good feedback is needed to demonstrate the relevance.

Tests may be combined with . . .

Watson Glaser to add a verbal reasoning dimension, and with Myers Briggs Type Indicator and OPQ for a more general personality profile.

Static/predictive value

Good, reliable, predictive value of conceptual ability, unlikely to change.

Overall review

Speed of being tested – 40 minutes timed, perhaps 1 hour untimed
Speed of scoring results – fast
Cost – low
Range of applications – intelligence test, conceptual thinking
In-house/Out-house – In-house, under licence
Basic/Advanced – advanced

How to prepare yourself for sitting this test

Intellectual efficiency, compared with intellectual capacity, is more dependent on physical and mental health, so it would be unwise to attempt Raven's and hope to score a high mark if the person doing the test was feeling unwell.

Familiarity with the test situation and practising completing tests tends to increase efficiency more than capacity, so those who have done Raven's before will have an advantage. (Of course, the more tests are used generally, the greater will be the incentive for people to familiarise themselves with the tests beforehand, and this is one of the purposes of this book.)

However, it is a typical procedure in tests with right or wrong answers such as Raven's Matrices, for the tester to ascertain if the person has practised with these tests before, and they may then decide to give the person being tested an alternative yet similar test, such as the GMA abstract test.

Coaching in practice and familiarisation is built into the Raven's Matrices, which minimises the advantage that people may have from having done the test before. Those overseeing the test being administered have been trained to look for people who have been coached, and are used to detecting those who have learned the correct answers. For those who know they will have to complete Raven's Matrices and wish to perform well it can be possible to practise by finding similar tests, but it is unlikely that you will be informed in advance of the particular version of the matrices you may be given.

Will this test produce a different result after a period of time?

As suggested above, a person's abstract reasoning ability reaches a peak in early teenage years, so it would be unlikely to be possible to produce an improved result after a period of time. On the contrary, the evidence suggests that abstract reasoning ability deteriorates, so a poorer result would be more likely after a number of years.

Watson Glaser Critical Thinking Analysis

Background

Although Watson Glaser is an ability rather than a personality test, it is included here because of its insight into critical reasoning skills, which can be vital in the selection process. It is one of the most well-known and well-established verbal reasoning tests, with the most recent version having been developed in 1977.

The aims of the test

The Watson Glaser Critical Thinking Analysis looks at patterns of intellectual thought according to five main areas:

Test 1 looks at inference;
Test 2 looks at the recognition of assumptions;
Test 3 looks at deduction;
Test 4 looks at interpretation; and
Test 5 looks at the evaluation of arguments.

The format

The Watson Glaser Critical Thinking Analysis is a test which includes 5 separate sets of problems, with 80 questions altogether. There is a large amount of text to read and digest at each point. The five tests examine five specific areas of critical thinking in turn, but all have a similar format.

Range of applications

Senior managerial roles, and especially used in selection for jobs seen to require extensive use of critical faculties.

Doing the test

Before each test there is an example, and then it is necessary to consider each new problem and make a decision. The Watson Glaser Test takes at least half an hour and could probably take longer if unlimited time was allowed, as such a large amount of time needs to be spent on reading and understanding the separate problems.

While doing the Watson Glaser Test, it is important not to lose one's train of thought, and there is a great need for concentration. The Watson Glaser Test is intellectually quite taxing and it can be difficult to achieve a high result without putting some effort into understanding each problem in turn. These are complex problems, with a strongly American flavour, but applicable to other contexts.

Examples of content of the test

(Not possible for copyright reasons.)

Time needed to complete the test

A strictly-timed 30-minute session is allowed.

Time needed to score the test

Quickly, can be done on the spot and the feedback given in the same session.

Necessary time for feedback

Between 20–30 minutes, or could be more if part of a selection procedure, when it could form the basis of a discussion.

Format/structure of the feedback

The feedback given after the test is related to the overall score, and sometimes according to individual performance in the five tests, one by one.

An overall percentile score is given of the total result. It is important to determine the norms by which the person is being measured, and these must be appropriate to their professional role.

Value to the employer/user

Watson Glaser is used a great deal in the selection of people in jobs requiring in-depth critical reasoning. There will be a band in which people will be either accepted or rejected, according to a specific percentile score.

Those with Watson Glaser results which are extremely high may well be seen as too overtly academic, but those who obtain low results may indicate a lack of critical reasoning and logical thinking.

Value to the employee/person being tested

Completing this test is extremely useful in analysing your capacity to deal with difficult verbal problems, and can open your eyes to being able to 'read between the lines' in a variety of contexts.

Value to the user organisation

Again, Watson Glaser, as in the case of the more basic personality tests, gives sound insight into the ability of a person to perform well in certain cultures. Many companies within the macho culture type use Watson Glaser, as do high-risk, slow-feedback companies, but it is less used in retail and process cultures. It is highly necessary in companies with a great need for high-powered individual intellectual performance in problem-solving and executing a variety of assignments, where lateral thinking is needed.

Can the test results be deliberately falsified?

With difficulty, and probably only through acquiring a copy of the test and practising, or learning the answers to fabricate results, but if the job requires a certain amount of intellectual horsepower which is lacking in the person attempting it, there would be no point in trying to get through a selection procedure this way, as the job itself would then be too taxing.

Advantages over other tests

The Watson Glaser Test is in great contrast to the standard personality tests, which really only test the type of person you are and require no intellectual input. Here, there is very definitely a right or wrong answer in each case.

Disadvantages compared with other tests

Looks only at critical reasoning, not other aspects of ability, and can be off-putting to a person who feels they haven't done well in it. Americanisms abound and all the examples are set in the USA, and this can be confusing to the UK reader.

Tests may be combined with . . .

Other verbal reasoning tests, with abstract tests such as Raven's Progressive Matrices, and personality tests such as OPQ and Myers Briggs Type Indicator.

Static/predictive value

Good static and predictive value, as results unlikely to change much.

Overall review

Speed of being tested – fairly fast
Speed of scoring results – fast
Cost – low
Range of applications – senior positions, and sometimes junior
In-house/Out-house – In-house, under licence
Basic/Advanced – advanced

How to prepare yourself for sitting this test

This needs brains and thought, so you must carefully read the instructions and gear yourself up for serious thinking. Try to make decisions as logically as possible, not based on instinct. Try to take this test at a time of day when you feel fresh and alert.

Will this test produce a different result after a period of time?

It is possible, but unlikely, especially after the age of 30. Ability to answer the test may improve after doing it a number of times, but it is unlikely that basic critical thinking capacity will change radically.

The Colour Test

Background

The Colour Test provides a glimpse below the surface of an individual, describing the background to their way of thinking, and has been included here as it analyses personality in a totally different way from any of the other tests considered in this book. The Colour Test is old established and has been used for several years, and goes through phases of being in and out of fashion. There is a concern that face validity is not high and the point of doing it at all has been questioned from time to time. However, its use is still sufficiently widespread for inclusion here, and it provides a useful contrast to the other, more psychometric personality tests.

The aims of the test

The test aims to examine individual personality traits and aspects of emotional development which can be indicative of the role of the individual within teams, and his or her emotional stability for senior executive roles. In the same way as the Insight Profile, emotionality is seen as underlying all the other aspects of personality, and capable of undermining or negating any of the others.

Many people have never thought of the use of choosing and arranging patterns of colours in this way, but they do have a remarkable role to play in basic and advanced psychology, and have been used for some time in psychological tests in different ways.

The format

In this test, the testee is asked to arrange a number of coloured tiles – in a total of 14 shades of colours – according to a few simple rules. The tiles are used to construct two pyramids, of equal size and shape. The important factor is the choice of colours and the number of each colour chosen, as well as the way in which they are arranged. The idea is to select the colours without too much prior thought and according to what appeals at the time.

Range of applications

As a basic personality test, and in selection, career development and team-role exercises, to augment psychometric personality tests.

Doing the test

The tiles are spread out in front of the person doing the test, and the wealth of different colours is offered equally. Then it is just a question of selecting the colours which appeal and arranging them within the pyramid. This is followed by in-depth feedback concerning the implications of the choices.

Examples of content of the test

Coloured tiles of 14 different colours, including primaries and colour mixes, with light and dark versions of each, which are arranged on a template of a pyramid shape.

Time needed to complete the test

About 10–15 minutes, overseen by the person administering the test.

Time to score the test

Within the feedback process; the test is scored as the implications of the choices are explained.

Necessary time for feedback

About 20–30 minutes.

Format/structure of the feedback

The resulting pattern from the arrangement of the tiles and, above all, the colours chosen can then be interpreted as a key to the subject's emotional makeup, showing up such aspects as a tendency towards personal frustration or a tendency to be over-intellectual, i.e. the preponderance of one aspect of someone's character. The Colour Test can show creativity, and attitude to structures and controls. This is explained in the context of the colours chosen.

Every colour, according to psychologists, has what they call a different 'stimulus content' and 'stimulus quality'. The coloured stimuli presented to the person doing the test evokes physiological and psychological reactions in terms of positive or negative attraction or repulsion, for varying lengths of time.

The three components of reaction involved in the Colour Test have been identified by psychologists by the concepts of what they define as:

excitation potential;
arousal value; and
affective content.

The **excitation potential** of a coloured stimulus may be strong or weak; its **arousal value** may be high leading to a sudden but quickly extinguished response, or it may be low resulting in a continuous and long-lasting response; and its **affective content** may vary between the poles of elation and depression.

An intermediate state between these three reactions also apparently exists for each component. Psychologists consider that every colour may be placed at one of these three levels.

The principle of analysing the choices of coloured tiles has been shown to be a useful and valid exercise, in both clinical and occupational settings. The choice of specific colours and the number of tiles of these colours chosen is thus indicative of broad personality categories.

The value of the Colour Test scheme becomes more apparent in the context of classifying emotional behaviour in terms of their excitation, arousal and affective content. This requires the categorising of three basic forms of emotional behaviour. These include the concepts of mood state, of being affected and of emotion.

A **mood state** represents the direction of emotionality predisposing the individual's expression of his or her needs and feelings.

The term **affect** is used to describe the brief, rapidly dissipated feeling which responds to internal or external stimulation and which may be associated with intensive arousal effects.

Emotion is used to classify a persisting state which may be associated with specific stimulus objects and contents. Mood states can be described in terms of their affective contents, i.e. they may vary from elation to depression. Affects may differ in arousal value, depending upon the positive or negative attributes of the associated stimulus objects.

This model treats colour choices entirely in terms of inferences with respect to the emotional aspects of personality. This is arbitrarily restrictive since it is recognised that other than emotional meanings may be associated with the different colours. Colour symbolism, folklore and art suggest that other meanings are indeed often associated.

The Colour Test provides an insight into some basic psychology of the control of emotion, which can vary from the free expression of all emotional feelings, to a striving for a stable and even rigid emotional balance. In extreme cases, where the dynamics of the emotional system break down, an individual can show a fixation of the emotional structure, where his or her mood state becomes rigid and no longer sensitive to its normal feedback mechanism. This situation arises in the psychoses and severe neurotic conditions. At the other extreme, there is an uncontrolled increase of 'excitation potential', where fluctuations of mood state occur which are totally unrelated to emotional content. In extreme forms of abnormal behaviour, shifts from extremely rigid to extremely open and uncontrolled emotional expression may also be expected.

Value to the employer/user

Overall the test has useful insights into emotional development and into attitudes to others in the workplace. It can be useful in understanding the emotional stability of employees, and the use of the Colour Test helps explain the factors underlying results shown from the less in-depth psychometric personality tests. If the basic psychometric personality tests are judged to be enough for the creation of teams, then there is no need to use the Colour Test or the DMT, but many employers are interested in probing beneath the surface.

Value to the employee/person being tested

This test can be quite an eye-opener in terms of explaining emotional development through choice of colours, and provides fascinating insight into why people have a particular outlook.

The psychology is quite advanced and not easy to understand when doing the test as a simple one-off exercise, but for those who have become interested in the role of psychology in their performance at work, the Colour Test provides a new dimension.

Value to the user organisation

Different emotional types will fit into different organisations, and basically the Colour Test reveals who has a need for structure, and who does not.

Macho cultures and high-risk, slow-feedback cultures require people without a great need for structure, and for those who are emotionally self-sufficient. Process and retail cultures are more group-oriented and offer a greater degree of support. Senior executives with a considerable degree of responsibility need to show a median level of emotionality (a point also discussed in the Insight Profile test).

Can the test results be deliberately falsified?

It would be possible to choose colours according to the impression which the person doing the test feels it is appropriate to convey, but this would negate the whole purpose of the exercise, and would almost certainly be detected in the feedback session.

Advantages over other tests

More insight into underlying psychology of the individual than the less in-depth psychometric tests, which are seen by many psychologists as superficial.

Disadvantages compared with other tests

Not having great face validity, some executives may see little point in doing this test, and a number of executive search consultants and personnel staff are wary of using this test as a result. Needs to be combined with other, more easily understandable, psychometric personality tests.

Tests may be combined with . . .

Can be used with the DMT, as a further insight into personality development and emotional background, to confirm the DMT's findings. For overall value, would need to be combined with more occupationally-oriented basic personality tests, such as OPQ and Myers Briggs Type Indicator. The Colour Test can help explain why a person has developed a specific personality type, and provide good background material for a further battery of tests.

Static/predictive value

Good predictive value, unless the mood state changes fundamentally (as discussed below). Useful as a static test, explaining existing personality traits.

Overall review

Speed of being tested – fast
Speed of scoring results – fast
Cost – medium
Range of applications – when need to go beyond basic tests
In-house/Out-house – In-house, under licence
Basic/Advanced – advanced

How to prepare yourself for sitting this test

It is not appropriate to try to think of the significance of certain colours and the implications of choosing these, but to opt for the colours which most appeal in an intuitive way, and to arrange them in a pleasing design which you find attractive. If you do not believe that the test has value, it would be better not to attempt it, rather than to do it without care or thought.

Will this test produce a different result after a period of time?

The total emotional system is seen by psychologists as a dynamic structure which will respond to internal and external stimuli. Therefore, the test could easily produce different results over a period of time. The individual's mood state will influence the expression of affect and emotions, but the feedback of affective and emotional experience may also serve to modify mood states.

According to the psychologists, this emotional system is by no means static, but may be modified as the result of what they call 'developmental sequences or critical experiences' within the life of the individual. The emotional balance of the child will differ from that of the adult, and the experience of trauma, physical insult or emotional crises will have different consequences on the emotional system.

The DMT

Background

The Defense Mechanism Test (DMT), developed by the Swedish psychologist Kragh in 1969, has now been evaluated by a number of other psychologists in Europe and the USA, who maintain that the best use of this test, for occupational applications, lies in its ability to help predict success in stressful occupations. This reflects the DMT's background in Freudian theory: Freud, in 1914, said that 'the theory of repression is the cornerstone on which the whole structure of psychoanalysis rests'. The theory of defences was revised extensively between 1895 and 1939, and was welded to the theories of development, neurosis, therapy, dreaming and art, among others. The DMT is quite different from the other tests profiled here in this book, in terms of the way it is administered and the insight it gives into the inner psychology of the individual. It is the most clinical (rather than occupational) of the tests included, but here is considered – as for the other tests profiled in this book – in the context of senior management selection and career development although, as we shall see, it has other applications, in sport and in military training.

The aims of the test

The DMT aims to provide detailed insights into an individual's emotional and psychological development, and in the occupational context gives a view of the person's ability to cope with stress, and facility to make judgements based on only partial information.

The format

The person undergoing the test is subjected to quite a strange experience, which can be both frustrating and illuminating at the same time. The individual looks into a metal box (like a seaside

funfair picture-show exhibit from the Victorian age), called a
tachitoscope, which blocks out all light except the pictures it projects, flashing at the viewer for very precise periods of time.

People doing the DMT are shown a slide very briefly – initially
for a very short fraction of a second – and are asked to report
verbally on, and draw what they see. Each person being tested is
given a large sheet of paper with 20 empty squares, to be filled in
with drawings of what seems to him or her to appear on the slide
each time. The way the individual reacts to the pictures is revealed
in the processes of reporting, and the drawings in the squares,
which become progressively more clearly-defined as the slides are
viewed for longer periods each time.

The pictures shown in the test involve several points of recognition, and the perception of these, in timing and detail, is used to
show quantifiably the results indicating the individual personality
development. Blips on the chart in the final scoring sheet can often
be closely matched with aspects of the individual's emotional life.

Range of applications

Clinical uses, and in occupational applications, in senior recruitment and career development exercises; can also be used in assessing trainees, in their ability to succeed in potentially stressful
occupations, and for how well individuals will work together in a
group or team.

Doing the test

The DMT is a frustrating yet illuminating experience, probably
quite different from anything previously encountered, even by
those familiar with psychological tests. The person doing the test
has a chance to understand how it works, by being given an opportunity for a dummy run.

The process of doing the actual DMT exercise is at the same
time slightly scary but fascinating. It is extremely difficult at the
beginning to draw anything in the squares, because you can see
very little, and you will be some way into the test before it is
possible to discern specific shapes. Still, it is necessary to draw
something at each showing of the slides, and you should not be
embarrassed or restrained by poor drawing ability. The psychol-

ogist will also ask you to explain verbally what you think you see each time.

Examples of content of the test

It would be against the DMT copyright to reveal the nature of the pictures being shown in the tachitoscope, and clearly this would mean that the test results could then be fabricated.

Time needed to complete the test

Probably around an hour, including introduction and familiarisation with this unusual test medium.

Time to score the test

The psychologist will take the drawings away for between 30 minutes and 1 hour, and will score the pictures according to the perception of certain features in the pictures at various stages in the test.

Necessary time for feedback

The DMT is part of a six-hour process of assessment when used at Pintab, and is included in feedback of the entire process. When being used separately, at least half an hour is needed, especially in terms of explaining the findings and relating them to the individual's personal background.

Format/structure of the feedback

This will involve explaining the implications of the findings, probably both in terms of the individual's personality and occupationally. Basically, the DMT provides a set of hypotheses about each person being tested, clearly indicating certain features about him or her:

- the DMT can show the way that anxiety and uncertainty is controlled and managed by the individual, and what level of defences are mobilised as a protection;

- the DMT reveals whether people have had to grow up early, with implications for their sense of responsibility;
- the DMT records activity or passivity, the propensity to integrate or remain apart, and the level of inner resilience of the individual.

Above all, the DMT – as a psychoanalytic rather than psychometric test, based on one-to-one, here and now, not compared with any given population – is significant in terms of registering defence mechanisms, speed of reaction and sensitivity/insensitivity. In spite of only partial information, can the subject hold on to reality? Senior people with a great deal of responsibility need to be able to think on their feet, act quickly and exhibit tenacity. Will the person continue to be a good middle manager, or could he or she go further, showing creativity, a high conceptual capacity and resilience?

When top CEOs are undergoing the DMT, the strength of their defence mechanisms are revealed; they may be overtaking others on the career ladder, but can they delegate and trust others? They may have strong technical dispositions, but can they work with others? The test reveals that they may see themselves as tough and assertive, or benign and supportive. They may see authority as threatening, or as sympathetic. Arguably, such qualities cannot be measured, and predictions of future performance made, in just a standard interview situation. Increasingly, in a number of large corporates in mainland Europe in particular, the DMT is helping senior human resources people to look beneath the surface in a totally novel way. The trend is being picked up more and more in the UK and the USA.

In giving feedback on the DMT, it is likely that the psychologist will attempt to explain the psychological background to the test. According to psychologist Paul Kline, the DMT claims to reveal important and forgotten experiences in a subject's life, using psychoanalytic definitions of defence mechanisms, which are seen to resemble Freudian defences, first described several decades ago. The DMT is also seen as a useful test in the clinical setting, although its main application has been occupational.

The DMT investigates the relationship between perception and personality by examining descriptions of stimuli. According to Kline, 'subjects draw the stimuli and label their descriptions. The changes and the transformations in the descriptions of the stimuli are claimed, *inter alia*, to reveal the defense mechanism used by subjects and reveal the past in the present.' Kline refers to a link between the series of descriptions of the stimuli and the psychological life-story of the person being tested.

There are many questions and doubts surrounding the use of the DMT. Does it measure the defences which it is claimed to do? Is it able to represent the past? What advantages can be obtained from presenting the testing material/format 'subliminally'? (arguably, the subliminal presentation does change the nature of the test, and gives access to personality data that could not be obtained by a simple, non-subliminal presentation of the same stimuli).

Kline argues that given that defences are widely applicable strategies adopted by the ego to deal with internal and external threats, and that the individual tends to employ the same types of defence in different situations, the operational defences used by the person in situations of uncertainty are likely to be mirrored in certain observable personality characteristics.

According to Kline, the most psychometrically acceptable personality questionnaires, such as a 16-PF and EPQ (devised by Eysenck) rely substantially on the honesty and insight of the person being tested, and may thus be unable to take account of unconscious motivation. In contrast, the designers of projective tests have tended to emphasise the importance of unconscious motivation in determining behaviour.

A separate study has been made of the DMT as a predictor of the behaviour of pilots in military flying. In its origins in Sweden, the DMT was developed partly because of the 40/60 pass/fail proportion of students beginning basic flight training with the Swedish Air Force. The DMT helped significantly in the study of how perception developed in these individual students. It also helped at the selection stage to define a group of pilot applicants who had a lower and higher risk than others of becoming failures in their flight training. The DMT helped identify those liable to adjustment difficulties in their working situation and problems in their relationships with their comrades, those liable to show psychosomatic symptoms and flight neuroses, and those likely to be more accident prone. Apparently, the use of the DMT in the selection procedure for the Swedish Air Force changed the pass/fail proportion from the earlier 40/60 to 60/40.

Psychologists argue that the defences used by an individual and the extent to which they are used are a stable characteristic of that person, based on personal life experiences. Results from the DMT can be generalised to all situations where the individual defends against anxiety.

Value to the employer/user

The DMT can be particularly useful in selecting employees for particular roles in the company, especially where they will have to make decisions under stress in conditions of uncertainty, and must be able to think on their feet. There are obvious applications in the financial services sector, and in senior positions with a large amount of responsibility. How would a person react to authority? What would be their attitude to subordinates? The DMT is an elaborate test, to be used selectively, either comparing a number of people, or to analyse a key senior person. The DMT gets below the surface to a much greater extent than most other psychological tests, but is also more time-consuming and expensive than most, and the point of doing it must be clearly appreciated.

Value to the employee/person being tested

This test can give the most amazing insights into personal develop ment, and can graphically explain the reasons behind your having a particular attitude and approach to work. The DMT can explain why you have particular strengths and weaknesses, and how they might be improved or offset. Of all the tests considered in this book, the DMT is potentially the most mind-blowing for the individual taking it. However, although you may feel that, through completing the DMT, you are laying your soul bare, the understanding gleaned by the psychologist is primarily used to make predictions about professional capacity and managerial behaviour at senior levels, as well as enhancing your understanding of your own personality.

Value to the user organisation

The DMT can be used in team-building, and in matching particular individuals to particular roles. It could also be used in matching senior individuals to certain corporate cultures, but probably there are quicker and less expensive ways of doing this.

Can the test results be deliberately falsified?

Almost certainly not, because what the person is being asked to do bears no relation to the overall psychological findings. There is no way of knowing how the test is scored, and how a person could prepare the drawings to show personality facets which were not there.

Advantages over other tests

The advantage of the DMT is that it is not a self-report test and the responses cannot be controlled by the individual at all: it is thus impossible to falsify. Therefore, it can reveal previously-hidden traits.

The DMT gives in-depth insight into personality (and history of personality development) to a greater degree than most other psychological tests. The DMT is incredibly probing, and most people doing the test are enormously impressed with the accuracy of the results and the way it is administered; clearly the enthusiasm and competence of the psychologist is very important.

Disadvantages compared with other tests

The DMT is comparatively expensive and time-consuming, and some executives may rebel against the idea of doing a test which does not appear to have high face validity, which seems strange and may make them feel uncomfortable. They may also feel that it is an invasion of privacy, and that their employer does not have a right to know so much about them.

Tests may be combined with . . .

The DMT has some similarities with the Omega Motivation and Competency Inventory, in terms of probing the individual's inner psyche, and could be combined with this to provide a very in-depth analysis of how an individual thinks, and why this individual came to think in this way. It is often combined with the Colour Test, Raven's Matrices and Watson Glaser to give an overall picture of personality and competence. As the DMT is really more clinical than occupational, it could be combined with simpler personality tests such as OPQ and PAPI, which would add more to the picture of the individual in a work setting.

Static/predictive value

The DMT is unusual in providing historical as well as current understanding, and is also useful in predicting particularly reliably how an individual will behave in the future, because it is based on researching back into the individual's development.

Overall review

Speed of being tested – slow
Speed of scoring results – slow
Cost – relatively high
Range of applications – clinical and occupational, selection and career development
In-house/Out-house – Out-house, with a licensed psychologist
Basic/Advanced – advanced

How to prepare yourself for sitting this test

You should prepare yourself to be surprised, even amazed, at what might be revealed, especially in terms of indicating aspects of your childhood and your emotional development.

Will this test produce a different result after a period of time?

Not substantially, because it is clearly not possible to change your past, but different experiences subsequently might produce a new development within the personality. This is not a test which could be completed more than once in five years, such is the novelty of the way it is presented.

Non-occupational note

The DMT is extensively used by sports stars, and is recommended by the British Olympic Association's psychology steering group. A series of athletes undertook the DMT. It has also been widely used in football teams. As psychologist Olya Khaleelee commented, 'it got to the point where the results could be used to determine which footballer should play where in the team, and that could raise ethical questions too'.

Belbin's Team Role Model Tests

Background

Management Teams International, based in East Grinstead, has developed what it calls 'a unique concept in business team management skills', based on the teachings of Dr Meredith Belbin. The company claims that its revolutionary new view of teams can improve management effectiveness by 20–30 per cent by enhancing the performance of individuals, and the balance and effectiveness of teams. Participants on their courses, they claim, can improve their personal performance by 10–15 per cent and participants learn how to build, modify and organise teams in their day-to-day business activities, improving their effectiveness by 10–15 per cent.

In the course of many years of research, Dr Belbin discovered nine specific team roles. All teams are made up of these, and there are no others. These roles can be predicted by psychometric tests and are a constant feature of each individual. People are classified according to their predominant type, together with their second and third type. Although all the team types are equally valuable in a team situation, some combinations are more effective than others. Each of the team types has allowable weaknesses which must be tolerated for the benefit of the strengths that go with them. The ideal is to concentrate on your strengths while tolerating the weaknesses of your own team type and that of others. By doubling or even trebling up different team roles in one individual, all the nine roles can be represented in a team of three or four people. The most successful team is one which combines a fair distribution of the different team types.

The aims of the test

Through participating in a seminar based on the Belbin model, this test aims to help people to have increased confidence in their own strengths, and to recognise and accept their weaknesses while acknowledging the strengths and weaknesses of others, and becoming more tolerant of colleagues previously regarded as unacceptable.

In the Belbin team role exercise, called 'Teamopoly', the team-role profiles of each team player come through very strongly. The exercise has been designed around fundamental business principles, including the need to cope with the present while managing with the future, understanding the role of finance, the value of personal relationships in negotiating and the importance of successful negotiating in business. The exercise was designed ideally for teams of four participants, eliminating elements of chance so that the lessons of success and failure are attributed to team differences more than to luck. There are no arbitrary decisions or changes during the exercise and it is easy to grasp what is involved while allowing ample opportunity for ploys. The exercise has been tested and implemented over the last 5 years and has been modified when necessary.

The game gives an opportunity for the teams to work on a realistic business problem, requiring financial acumen and administrative skills, awareness of logistic detail, speed of response, quick decision-making, appraisal of a competitive situation, negotiating skills, ability to utilise market research, administrative efficiency and attention to detail, ability to understand exact specifications, understanding of different financial strategies (including secured loans, unsecured loans, and venture capital), tax management, and rapid grasp of detail and an ability to think on your feet. No one is allowed to work on their own but has to join in with their team. It is necessary to work to close deadlines, keeping all the issues under control. The game continues for $1\frac{1}{2}$ days, and clearly exhibits the different team roles in action. The game has been improved and modified over three years of use.

The format

The test – in one of its forms – involves attending a two day seminar, in which the team type variants are explained in detail. Before arriving at the seminar venue, the participants have completed self-assessments and arranged observer assessments. The first day begins with an introduction and explanation, and then the participants are divided into groups and play 'Teamopoly', a specially-designed game to test the behaviour of particular teams. The performances of the teams are then appraised.

Range of applications

In team-building and career development, of middle-managers in particular, but also applicable to more senior executives. Not necessarily used in selection.

Doing the test

The process of doing the Belbin exercise begins with the classification of participants into particular team roles, as a result of their having filled in a 'self-perception' assessment, and having asked colleagues to complete 'observer' assessments. In the self-perception inventory, prospective participants answer a series of questions arranged in 7 categories, totalling 10 in each. Each section consists of statements which are apportioned a weighting according to their respective importance, and each section must add up to 10 points (see 'Examples of content of the test', page 195).

The prospective participant in the team roles exercise is then asked to approach six colleagues and ask them to fill in an observer's assessment sheet, containing two lists of descriptive words. List A contains 45 words, generally favourable; List B includes 27 words, generally negative. The observer is asked to tick the most appropriate words to a total of not more than 33 in List A, and not more than 19 in List B. These assessments help to develop an overall picture of your team type. The Belbin model is unique in asking people not just how they would report on themselves, but also in building up a picture of how others see them.

The research conducted by Dr Meredith Belbin is based around dividing people up into specific team types. Why did he decide to do this, and what is the justification for the team roles approach?

Management Teams International argues that the search for successful management has been seen almost exclusively as a search for the right individual.

Yet, arguably, the ideal individual cannot ever be found, because the ideal individual does not exist, and cannot exist. Too many of the qualities in an ideal manager are mutually exclusive:

- being highly intelligent yet not too clever;
- forceful yet sensitive;
- dynamic yet patient;
- able to communicate yet able to listen;
- decisive yet reflective; and so on.

Also, a problem with ideal individuals is that they can be easily lost to competitors, or enter a new field, or otherwise leave the business: investing everything in the individual is having too many eggs in one basket.

Thus, Management Teams International suggests that the building of a successful team can ensure a range of ideal qualities and a degree of continuity. However, teams can be successful or unsuccessful, and the research of Dr Meredith Belbin since 1969 has, to a large extent, shown why. By studying many teams in action and through using a battery of different psychometric tests, a number of management team hypotheses began to emerge. These were tested over several years, so that ultimately Dr Belbin was able to predict the success of specific teams during a business game, by simply looking at the team types combination, without even interviewing the members of the teams.

The seminar looks at the nine team types in some detail. The nine team roles are: co-ordinator, shaper, plant, resource investigator, team-worker, implementer, monitor/evaluator, completer finisher, specialist.

Co-ordinators tend to be mature, confident and make a good chair-person figure. They clarify goals and promote decision-making, but they are not necessarily the most clever or creative member of a group. They are best fitted to be leaders of the team and to preside over its combined efforts. Co-ordinators are preoccupied with objectives and have a substantial degree of 'character'. They are disciplined, authoritative and often charismatic, although not domineering. They are free from jealousy and delegate readily, without pride of authorship. Co-ordinators see clearly the roles of the other members of the team, operating through consultation with control. They are neither too talkative nor too quiet, and are good at asking questions and making proposals. They are competent at summing up the results of a meeting and taking decisions firmly.

Shapers are dynamic, outgoing, dominant, extrovert, and can be highly strung and anxious. They challenge, pressurise and find their way around obstacles, but can be prone to provocation, and short-lived bursts of temper. Shapers are task leaders and complement the role of the co-ordinator, who may be seen as the overall social leader. If there is no co-ordinator, shapers will almost automatically take charge. They have a great need for achievement and are impatient; they can feel paranoid, but they do not harbour grudges. Headstrong and assertive, they can show strong emotional response to frustration or disappointment. Shapers put more of their own personal input into each situation than do co-ordinators. They thrive under pressure and don't mind taking unpopular decisions. They like to move forward urgently to action and are strongly geared to results. Shapers sometimes see the team as an extension of their ego and are intolerant of vagueness. They make the team uncomfortable but achieve results, even at the cost of appearing arrogant and abrasive.

Plants are so-called because they could be planted into an uninspired team to improve its performance. They carry the seeds of ideas, with a strong degree of originality and radicalism. Plants are creative, imaginative, unorthodox and can solve difficult problems, but they are often weak in communicating with and managing ordinary people. Plants tend to work in an unorthodox and unusual way, separate from the other members of the team. They are more concerned with fundamentals than details, and are thrusting and uninhibited in a way uncharacteristic of most introverts. They can be offended if their ideas are criticised. There is a danger that a plant's ideas may not fit in with the team's needs and objectives, and they may find it hard to explain themselves to those on a different wavelength. Plants can provide a vital spark, but it often needs a good co-ordinator to get the best out of them.

Resource investigators are extrovert, enthusiastic and communicative, exploring opportunities and developing contacts. They are likeable, sociable and gregarious, with an interest that is easily aroused, yet can be quickly lost once the initial wave of enthusiasm has evaporated. They are good at communicating with people both inside and outside of the company, and are natural negotiators. They bring information back to the group and are constantly on the move or on the telephone. They are ideal salespeople, diplomats and liaison people, and although they are good at new ideas, they lack the radical creativity of plants. Resource investigators can get bored without stimulus, but are active under pressure. They keep the team in touch with reality, although they must be encouraged to follow up on tasks agreed.

Implementers are disciplined, reliable, stable, controlled, conservative and efficient. They are practical organisers, turning ideas into actions. They are concerned with reality and what is feasible, and operate in a logical manner with a high degree of integrity, commitment and stability. However, they are inflexible and slow to respond to new possibilities, and can be upset by a sudden change of plan. They like structures and systems, and try to build these when they don't exist. Implementers like schedules and organisations charts, but reject speculative ideas which can't be pinned down. Implementers can be counted upon to do reliably what needs to be done, even if no one else wants to do it. If anyone does not know what has been decided at the end of a meeting, he or she would most likely go to the implementer to find out.

Monitor evaluators are also highly intelligent, but are more sober, strategic and discerning than plants. They are also introverted, but more stable and aware of all the options. Monitor evaluators are serious and prudent, but lack the ability and drive to inspire others. Their contribution is measured and dispassionate, and they can stop the team from making major mistakes. They are constructively critical without letting their ego cloud their judgement. They can assimilate large amounts of material objectively and can assess the contributions of others. They must not be allowed to act as a damper on the team, yet it must be appreciated that they play a key role at crunch decision time.

Completer finishers are painstaking, conscientious and determined to deliver error-free work on time. They are introverted, anxious and reluctant to delegate, and are never satisfied until everything has been checked. They have a great capacity for follow through and attention to detail, and will not start something they can't finish. Although unassertive, they communicate a permanent sense of urgency, and insist on discipline and focus. Completer finishers are obsessed with meeting deadlines and can depress the rest of the team with their anxiety about details. However, their relentless follow-through is ultimately crucial to the team's success.

Team workers are very sociable, sensitive, mild, perceptive and accommodating. They listen, build relationships and avoid friction, clearly perceiving the emotional undercurrents operating within the group. They make it their business to know about the private lives and families of the rest of the team, and are good at communicating concern and care. They can adapt easily to different situations and people, and are low in dominance and assertiveness. Team workers reinforce existing team ideas rather than demolishing or rivalling them. They promote unity and harmony between the more outgoing members of the team, avoiding confrontation and offering sympathy, understanding, loyalty and support. They may be indecisive, but they can hold the team together and their contribution becomes especially obvious when they are not around.

Specialists are brought into the team to contribute on a narrow front. They are single-minded, self-starting and dedicated, providing knowledge or technical skills in short supply, but their priorities are geared towards their specialisms rather than to the benefit of the team as a whole. They maintain professional standards and defend their own field, showing great pride in their specialism. They have great aptitude and can provide insight into a rare skill upon which the firm's product or service is based, and command support and respect because of their knowledge. However, specialists can be apart from some of the more dynamic elements of the team and can lack interest in other people's concerns.

Then when the team types are explained, the 'Teamopoly' game begins. Basically, in the 'Teamopoly' exercise, each team endeavours to run its business more successfully than its rivals and make greater profits. Teams have to explain their strategy, position and result at the end of the exercise. To appear as equal as possible, the teams will have the same number of participants at the same level.

The exercise requires the teams to be composed of those of a similar team role type, to create teams of identifiable character. This magnifies the strengths and weaknesses of the particular team type which predominates in each. The **red team** is usually composed of shapers and resource investigators. The **blue team** is composed of completer finishers and implementers. The **green**

team is mostly team workers and specialists, and the **yellow team** is mostly plants and monitor evaluators.

Thus, the red team is full of aggressive people battling for position; the blue team is composed of dedicated completer finishers who nevertheless lack leadership and ideas; the green team is dominated by amiable team worker types lacking drive and decisiveness; and the yellow team is full of intellectuals who beaver away without necessarily achieving a result. Nevertheless, any one of these teams can and do win the exercise, and come out with the most money at the end of the day.

The team-roles exercise, after a discussion of the various team types, begins with a long discussion period and then three cycles of actually playing the team game, 'Teamopoly'. This involves a degree of frenetic activity, encouraged by tight deadlines. At the end of each cycle, teams are encouraged to discuss their progress and their financial performance is posted up for the others to see. The teams are supervised by facilitators, observing the teams in action, and noting behaviour.

The behaviour of the individual teams in the exercise is very much determined by the predominant team type. In one particular exercise conducted by Jeff Hayden of Management Teams International in East Grinstead, comprising a mixed group of people from several different organisations, the participants were divided into the four teams and behaved in the way expected from their predominant team types. The red team, dominated by shapers and resource investigators, were particularly keen on winning and everyone wanted to contribute all the time. They were enthusiastic and noisy, and there was a constant shift in the leadership role between the different members of the team. The person taking the initiative at the beginning of the exercise was not the person leading the team at the end. There was a concern about getting a clear understanding from the outset and deciding on everyone's roles, although subsequently people did not stick to the roles they had been given. There was a lot of interest in future planning and negotiating. This team was very competitive, outgoing and aggressive.

The blue team was fairly conservative but keen on getting on with the task in hand. It was operating efficiently but there was little contingency planning if something went wrong. There was a lot of interest in what other teams were doing and thinking of strategies. There were some ideas, but a lack of a defined strategy with constant concern over the lack of a leader. Similarly, there was no one to monitor and evaluate the ideas, so this team spent a lot of time considering alternatives, most of them impractical.

The green team spent all their time together, never acting independently from each other, and often failed to come to an agreement. There was a certain lack of drive to achieve the objectives and a greater interest in staying together whatever happened.

Finally, the yellow team worked in silence on the individual jobs they had to do. They had a highly intellectual approach to the task and some members never spoke at all. There was a concern that everything must be thought through carefully, and the exercise˙ was being taken seriously for the sake of the game.

During this particular exercise, some companies had sent along two or three people who ended up in different teams. These people tended to congregate together during the coffee breaks, perhaps to the detriment of the other participants, who were on their own.

Examples of content of the test

In the self-assessment questionnaire, Section 1 asks, 'What I believe I can contribute to a team'; Section 2 asks, 'If I have a possible shortcoming in teamwork it could be the following . . .'; Section 3 asks, 'When I am involved in a project with other people . . .'; Section 4 asks, 'My characteristic approach to group work is that . . .'; Section 5 asks, 'I gain satisfaction in a job because . . .'; Section 6 asks, 'If I am suddenly given a difficult task with limited time and unfamiliar people'; and, Section 7 asks, 'With reference to the problems I experience when working in groups'.

The idea behind 'Teamopoly' is that each team becomes a company, and has to buy product components from the market and from other companies to make finished products to sell back to the market or to other companies for a profit. The winning company is the one with the most money at the end of the game. Each company has to submit its asset sheet at the end of each of three cycles.

Each company is given cash and product components, and is given the opportunity to buy more components by auction or by tender. More components can also be bought from other companies, for money or exchange. The auctions are held at a different place each time, and an important part of the game is to understand, from a series of clues, where the auction is being held.

Time needed to complete the test

Initially, the self-assessment takes about 20 minutes, and then the seminar, including the 'Teamopoly' game, takes $2\frac{1}{2}$ days.

Time to score the test

The self-assessment and observer assessment forms are computer-scored, and the feedback is given during the seminar.

Necessary time for feedback

Within the $2\frac{1}{2}$ day seminar.

Format/structure of the feedback

Before completing the 'Teamopoly' exercise, each person becoming involved with Belbin team types and with Management Teams International, is asked to complete a self-perception form, and must ask six colleagues to fill in observer forms, as well.

These are then assessed in terms of the results listing team types. These can vary significantly between varying observers, and of course from the person doing the test as well. For example, one individual (the author) perceived herself in this order: plant, resource investigator, shaper, completer finisher, implementer, specialist, monitor evaluator, co-ordinator, with team worker ranking last. Observers completing the observation forms saw her as, in ranked order: (i) shaper, resource investigator, plant; (ii) shaper, specialist, monitor evaluator; (iii) resource investigator, implementer, team worker; (iv) resource investigator, plant, specialist; (v) shaper, monitor evaluator, specialist; (vi) specialist, shaper, completer finisher. The overall ranking of the seven views of the team roles of this person was resource investigator, shaper, specialist, plant, completer finisher, implementer, monitor evaluator, co-ordinator and team worker. Thus in this particular instance, there were considerable discrepancies between perceived roles and observed roles. These assessments then form the basis of the division of the participants into teams. The performance of the teams in action is analysed at the end of the 'Teamopoly' game, according to the findings of the facilitators. The computer-scored self-assessments and observer assessments are given to the participants.

At the end of the 'Teamopoly' exercise, the teams discuss their experiences and what they have learned. It is emphasised that the team may have lost, but the individual will have always gained from the experience. Although the exercise may be carried out in-house for members of the same company, it can be better to put strangers together, and certainly existing real-life teams should not operate as teams in the exercise, since failure in the exercise may undermine their ability to work together in the future.

Extensive validation has been carried out by companies using the team-type profiles and sending people to play the 'Teamopoly' game, such as British Telecom and Philips Electronics. The exercise has already been carried out at Templeton College, Oxford, and in the USA, France, Australia and Scandinavia

Value to the employer/user

The Belbin model is useful in team construction, although the model ignores the fact that it can be important to have certain specialists with particular skills in each team too. A team could well need a finance director, a marketing manager and various technical experts, and these may or may not fit into the best combinations of Belbin types. It can be a luxury to have the ideal people to choose from, people ideal for that particular team but also representing a good combination of Belbin types. Thus it is an idealistic yet valuable concept, and is best used as a team integration device, for understanding the strengths and weaknesses of colleagues.

Value to the employee/person being tested

Unlike most other psychological tests, the Belbin exercise gives people the chance to analyse how they work with others, rather than seeing themselves in isolation. Doing this test makes you think much more about others, and their role in your team, than most other tests. It becomes clear that all team types are mutually dependent, and none can operate effectively on their own. Playing the 'Teamopoly' game is a real eye-opener to the way that team types work in practice, and can significantly affect your outlook when you return to your 'real' working environment.

A number of comments have been made by participants of the team roles exercise, including the following remarks: 'I learned all the things about myself which I have been trying to hide in the closet for the past 39 years, but I console myself by knowing that many other people felt the same' and 'after two days with these people I did find them a pain in the backside. Having had time to reflect on the experience, and realising we were all of a similar type, I now accept that others must find me a pain too!'

Value to the user organisation

The Belbin concept is very useful in team-building and career development, and could be further developed, especially in terms of combinations of roles. Which combinations can be favourable or unfavourable? Which combinations fit in well in certain corporate cultures? For example, a shaper/plant can be a problem combination, and there would be a need to choose the host culture very carefully. A shaper/completer is a very good type which focuses on the task and is good at leading the project. Co-ordinator/implementers can be good at achieving the objectives.

Can the test results be deliberately falsified?

Although the self-assessment forms could be falsified, the observer forms must be completed by others, and it would be impossible to carry out the 'Teamopoly' exercise pretending to be a different team type.

Advantages over other tests

Overall, the Belbin team roles present an entirely new approach to a dynamic and practical view of psychological testing. It is a novel, innovative idea which is simple but effective, and is still relatively under-used, although now quite well known. The exercise clearly exhibits the value of creating a balanced team and understanding the roles of people in it. It breaks away from the idea of personality tests being exclusively geared towards studying individuals in isolation.

Disadvantages compared with other tests

Clearly, it is not possible to achieve a perfectly balanced team in the Belbin mould in every working situation. Only companies with a large workforce developing new teams can experiment freely, although clearly existing teams could be modified to leverage the value of combinations of team types. So, this test may be theoretical rather than practical for some. Also, it takes a long time (how many managers or executives could give up $2\frac{1}{2}$ days to play games?) and is thus expensive. The team types can be analysed by other tests and looked at without playing the game, but the game is an essential part of the process.

Tests may be combined with . . .

A person's team type and subsidiary types can also be assessed through the OPQ test, which may give a different perspective. It could also be carried out with other approaches to teams, such as Woodcock's (see below).

Static/predictive value

Belbin is very useful in defining a person's current team type and seeing how this works in action, so the predictive qualities are explored as part of the exercise itself.

Overall review

Speed of being tested – slow
Speed of scoring results – slow
Cost – high (although one can do individual test on its own for £35 plus VAT per person)
Range of applications – team-building, career development
In-house/Out-house – Out-house at Management Teams International, or the company can conduct the exercise In-house for a client
Basic/Advanced – advanced

How to prepare yourself for sitting this test

You must be willing to go along with the game and 'willingly suspend disbelief' for it to be effective, co-operating with others as required. You must pretend you are in a real working situation.

The self-assessment forms should be completed as candidly as possible, or they may conflict with the type in action. You must try and overcome inhibitions and get involved, or the exercise would be a waste of time. It is important not to try and pretend that you are a different type, but just get involved in the game for its own sake.

Will this test produce a different result after a period of time?

It may do, if the person has been given different responsibilities in the meantime, but doing the test a second time would give a person an unfair advantage over others, because they would already know how the game worked and would not have to spend time learning it.

WOODCOCK'S TEAM DEVELOPMENT APPROACH: AN ALTERNATIVE TO BELBIN

A contrasting view of team development has been presented by Mike Woodcock in his *Team Development Manual*. This is a way of integrating interpersonal dynamics, and is especially useful in explaining why friction is caused between people. Woodcock concentrates on diagnosing teamwork problems, rather than looking at team types as such. He subscribes to a concept of creating teams in harmony. This concept for the success of teams is not necessarily widely adhered to; some users of teamwork models deliberately create conflict and aggression in composing teams, encouraging the criticism and challenging of ideas. Woodcock, on the other hand, believes that if people get on well the work of the team will be much improved.

Woodcock, in diagnosing teamwork problems, proposes a set of characteristics associated with a mature team. He defines nine characteristics, known as the 'the building blocks of effective teamwork'. These are:

    clear objectives and agreed goals;
    openness and confrontation;
    support and trust;
    co-operation and conflict;

sound procedures;
appropriate leadership;
regular review;
individual development; and
sound inter-group relations.

To understand team strengths and weaknesses, Woodcock has devised a questionnaire of 108 statements, of which an equal number relate to the 9 characteristics. In terms of the team as a whole, each statement can be true or false. This reveals the extent to which the building blocks or effectiveness have been achieved. From this point onwards, other procedures can be taken to solve the problems of the team. Woodcock is less interested in team types and is more concerned about how the team works in practice, and can thus be a useful adjunct to the Belbin model. Examples of statements within the building blocks questionnaire are taken at random:

'Decisions seem to be forced upon us'
'We seldom question the content or usefulness of our
    meetings'
'People do not say what they really think'
'Some of the managers are not trusted'
'There is mistrust and hostility'
'Inappropriate people make the decisions'
'Help is not forthcoming from other parts of the organisation'
'There are too many secrets'
'Conflicts are avoided'
'Disagreements fester'
'The accepted order is rarely challenged'
'In this team it pays to keep your mouth shut'
'People are not prepared to put their true beliefs upon the
    table'
'We should discuss our differences more'
'Our leader does not make the best use of us'
'We should take more account of how others see us' and
'The organisation as a whole is not a happy place to work in'.

Use of this questionnaire is helpful in analysing common characteristics of teams, defined by Woodcock as building blocks of effective teamwork.

The Bortner Type A Questionnaire

Background

People with only a cursory interest in psychology know about Type A and Type B personalities. The Bortner Type A Questionnaire is a short, easy exercise, high on face validity. It is often included in batteries of other personality tests, to confirm the trends suggested in other instruments, and to give a rating of the extent to which a person has a Type A personality or Type B personality. This instrument was originally devised to test people who are likely or unlikely to suffer from heart disease. It was discovered that Type A people were more likely to become coronary patients than Type B people. It was originally developed by Bortner after analysing hospital patients, and the most recent version was adapted by Cooper. It is now used in both clinical and occupational contexts.

The aims of the test

This well-known, simple instrument is used to test the extent to which a person has a Type A or Type B personality. This provides a simple insight for an employer into the people in the organisation who may be subject to stress, i.e. those who are Type A. Some will be higher on the scale than others and, although these Type A characteristics are generally prized qualities in an organisation, they can lead to conflict and instability. It can be useful to be able to build teams and groups based on a precise knowledge of employees' personality types.

The format

The test comprises a single sheet of paper with Type A statements listed on the left, and Type B statements listed on the right. The numbers 1–11 are spread across the space between each pair of statements, and the person completing the test simply circles the most appropriate one in each case. There are 14 pairs of statements.

Range of applications

This test is suitable for any selection or management development exercise, and can be used on any person at any level in an organisation. It is extremely general in nature, and is not necessarily occupationally-oriented.

Doing the test

It is simply a case of considering each pair of statements and deciding which is most true about yourself. If you are positive that the statement to the right – the Type A statement – exactly describes you, then circle 11. If you think it's mostly true, then circle 8 or 9. If the statements on the left more accurately reflect your personality, then you will be choosing lower numbers, but these will vary. Overall, most people fall clearly into one of the two camps, and it is just a question of the extent to which the statements apply to each individual.

Examples of content of the test

So, what are the differences between Type A people and Type B people? The test lists statements which suggest the following conclusions about Type A and Type B people, and the person completing the test simply decides which are most appropriate in each of the cases:

- Type A people tend never to be late for appointments whereas Type B people are fairly casual about them;
- Type A people are very competitive whereas Type Bs are not;
- Type As often anticipate what others are going to say in conversation, by nodding and attempting to finish the sentence for them, while Type Bs are good listeners;
- Type A people are always rushed and Type B people never feel rushed, even when under pressure;

- Type As are always impatient when they are waiting while Type Bs can usually wait patiently;
- Type As try to do many things at once, and are constantly thinking about what they will do next, while Type Bs take things one at a time;
- Type As are emphatic in speech, and fast and forceful in manner, while Type Bs are slow, deliberate talkers;
- Type As always want to do a good job which will be recognised as such by others, while Type Bs care more about satisfying themselves, no matter what others may think;
- Type As are fast moving in their habits and especially in walking and eating, whereas Type Bs are slow doing things;
- Type As are hard-driving in terms of pushing themselves and others, while Type Bs are much more easy-going;
- Type As tend to hide their feelings, whereas Type Bs will express them;
- Type As will have few interests outside of their work; whereas Type Bs will have many outside interests;
- Type As tend to be very ambitious and eager to get things done, whereas Type Bs are unambitious and casual.

It is fairly simple to define which personality type you are and to what extent, by adding up the scores given against each statement. Taking each of the above variables, simply score yourself from 1 to 11, according to which best reflects the way you behave in your everyday life, particularly at work (here we are looking at the use of this test in an occupational context). For example, if you are generally on time for appointments (in the first pair of statements), you should indicate a number between 7 and 11. If you are casual about appointments, you should indicate a number between 1 and 5.

Time needed to complete the test

Only between 5 and 10 minutes, perhaps even less, as the test comprises only 14 choices. It could take longer if the person answering the test is unsure of the extent to which they are Type A or Type B, as each statement has a scale of 11 options.

Time to score the test

This is quickly done, and is just a question of adding up the scores, the number circled against each statement. A Type B person would score between 14 and 84, whereas a Type A person would score between 85 and 154. Scoring a number between each type is quite rare.

Necessary time for feedback

Only about 10 minutes would be required to explain what is a very simple, self-explanatory test, but some of the statements are thought-provoking, and it can be useful to spend some time on these, especially as part of a career development exercise, when this test is used as a basis for discussion of behaviour.

Format/structure of the feedback

In the feedback, you may be asked for practical examples to confirm you choice of scores. If the psychologist or person providing feedback knows you well, he or she will have anticipated your choices. You may be asked which you think are good or bad characteristics, and why. You may be asked which you think are most helpful in the work context, and those which are not conducive to your success in the organisation. Have any of these qualities resulted in particular problems in your work? How do you work with people of the other type? Do they frustrate you (if you are a Type A person), or confuse, tire or baffle you (if you are a Type B person)?

Value to the employer/user

Most people fall clearly into one of the two types. Type As tend to be more stressed than Type Bs, although it is also a question of how the stress is handled (which is not necessarily shown in the Bortner test, but is shown in Sweney's Stress Index which picks up aspects of behaviour and lifestyle that usefully adds to the results of other tests).

It can be very useful to the employer to know the tendency towards Type A or Type B of staff, from junior people through to executives, especially in the formation of teams, and in analysing the success of particular individuals working together.

Value to the employee/person being tested

For a Type A person, this test may help you to realise why you get stressed at times, and can focus your attention on areas where you can try to offset the effects of stress. Why are you always rushed? Wouldn't it be possible to leave more time to make appointments and meet deadlines? Why are you always impatient while waiting? Couldn't you accept that sometimes you have to wait, you can't do anything about it, and use the time just to read or think through a problem? Perhaps you should try to eat less quickly, and not rush around the place quite so much. Perhaps you should learn to express your feelings more often, and not keep them bottled up so much? Perhaps you should try to do one thing at a time, and not start something new until you have finished the previous task, and not drive yourself quite so hard. Do others rebel at being pushed quite so much? Try looking at the situation from their point of view. Many Type A people would find it useful to develop interests outside of their job, so that they become slightly less obsessed about achieving at all costs.

For Type B people, the test is useful in highlighting areas where they could show more energy and drive. Should they be rather less casual about appointments, and make a greater effort not to be late? Should they take more interest in what others think in terms of their attitudes to tasks, as satisfying themselves may not be enough? Perhaps they should try to speed up their work, to get more done? Type Bs tend to have many outside interests from work: are they sure these are not detracting from their commitment to their job? Does their casual nature and approach mean that they are being overlooked for interesting and worthwhile opportunities?

Value to the user organisation

Again, the Bortner Type A Questionnaire is another useful exercise for fitting people into particular organisations, according to their cultures and styles. Some company cultures attract primarily Type As (such as the macho and work hard/play hard or retail cultures) and some tend to have a large proportion of Type

Bs (such as the process and high-risk, slow-feedback cultures). The results are also useful in developing individual teams, which need a mix of personality types.

Can the test results be deliberately falsified?

Clearly, if you want to present yourself as a Type A personality and you are something of a Type B (or vice versa) it would be easy to answer the test in a totally different way, but it would soon become obvious in your behaviour and approach if you had falsified the test. This would then reflect badly on your level of personal integrity, which would be damaging to the individual. Obviously, the most simple tests are the easiest to falsify, but also attempts to falsify them are the most transparent.

Advantages over other tests

It is simple, quick and gives a clear category rating, useful for both selection and management development exercises, and good as a discussion starter.

Disadvantages compared with other tests

Very simple, not in-depth, could be easily falsified and only shows limited insights. Not complete in itself in terms of giving a picture of an individual.

Tests may be combined with . . .

Could be combined with Sweney's Stress Index to give an added dimension to the areas an individual may see as stressful. Would probably confirm Sweney's Stress Index findings. Could be combined with more detailed tests, such as the OPQ personality series, as a 'taster' at the start of a series of tests. Could be given to someone who has never attempted a personality test before, to settle them into a long battery of tests. Could probably be usefully combined with any battery of personality tests, and can be used clinically, as well as occupationally.

Static/predictive value

It can be very difficult to change your basic personality type, but it may be that the extent to which you are a Type A or Type B could change with change of job or company.

Overall review

Speed of being tested – fast
Speed of scoring results – fast
Cost – low
Range of applications – wide
In-house/Out-house – either
Basic/Advanced – basic

How to prepare yourself for sitting this test

The test is not intellectually stretching or taxing, and just requires straightforward and honest answers which reflect your personal characteristics as accurately as possible.

You should not worry about right or wrong answers and trying to come over as a specific type; both Type A and Type B people have valuable roles to play in business and in organisations.

Will this test produce a different result after a period of time?

Possibly, as Type A people may become more stressed or less with a change in job, and Type B people may become more laid-back or less. But the basic types are unlikely to change. In the case of Type A personalities who are suffering undue stress, the Bortner Type A Questionnaire could be used in combination with Sweney's Stress Index after about a year or so, to see if efforts to reduce stress have been successful.

Useful Addresses

Test publishers

NFER Nelson Publishing Company Ltd, Darville House, 2 Oxford Road East, Windsor, Berkshire S14 1DF (Tel: 0753 858961)

Oxford Psychologists Press Ltd, Lambourne House, 311–21 Banbury Road, Oxford OX2 7JH (Tel: 0865 510203)

Saville and Holdsworth, 3 AC Court, High Street, Thames Ditton, Surrey KT7 0SR (Tel: 081-398 4170)

Testing companies

Management Teams International, Vacuna, Eden Vale, East Grinstead, West Sussex RH19 2JJ (Tel: 0342 870320)

Omega Management Consultants, 12 Queens Grove, St Johns Wood, London NW8 6EL (Tel: 071-586 5848)

PA Consulting Group, 123 Buckingham Palace Road, London SW1W 9SR (Tel: 071-730 9000)

Pintab Associates, Pepys House, 12 Buckingham Street, London WC2N 6DF (Tel: 081-202 7097)

Redfield Consulting Ltd, 2 Redfield Lane, London SW5 0RG (Tel: 071-373 4251)

Whitehead Mann Limited, Audit and Assessment Centre, 50 Welbeck Street, London W1M 7HE (Tel: 071-935 8978) *also*

McKenzie Davey, 16 Kent Terrace, Regents Park, London
NW1 6RP (Tel: 071-724 0330)

Pearn Kandola Downs, 76 Banbury Road, Oxford OX2 6JT
(Tel: 0865 516202)

Executive search firms using testing (referred to in this book)

Sarch Search International, 63–5 Marylebone Lane, London
W1M 5GB (Tel: 071-935 1155)

Succession Planning Associates, 26 Chapter Street, London
SW1P 4ND (Tel: 071-630 8080)

Miscellaneous

British Psychological Society, St Andrews House, 48 Princess
Road East, Leicester LE1 7DR (Tel: 0533 549568)

Independent Assessment and Research Centre, 57 Marylebone
Street, London W1N 3AE (Tel: 071-486 6106)

Institute of Personnel Management, Camp Road, Wimbledon,
London SW19 2AB (Tel: 081-946 9100)

Further Reading

Management and occupational psychology

M Devine, *The Photo-Fit Manager: Building a Picture of Management in the 1990s*, Unwin (1990)

Charles Handy, *Gods of Management*, Pan (1979)

E P Hollander, *Leadership Dynamics*, The Free Press, US (1978)

Antony Jay, *Management of Machiavelli*, Hodder and Stoughton (1969)

C Lewis, *Employee Selection*, Hutchinson (1985)

H Mintzberg, *The Nature of Managerial Work*, Harper and Row, US (1973)

M Reddy, *The Manager's Guide to Counselling at Work*, Methuen (1990)

M Smith and I T Robertson, *Systematic Staff Selection*, Macmillan (1986)

P B Warr, *Psychology at Work*, Penguin (1971)

Testing in general

A Anastasi, *Psychological Testing*, Macmillan (6th edn 1988)

L J Crombach, *Essentials of Psychological Testing*, Harper and Row (1984)

P Herriot, *Assessment and Selection in Organisations*, Wiley (1989)

Institute of Personnel Management, *The IPM Code on Psychological Testing*, IPM (1989)

David Keirsey and Marilyn Bates, *Please Understand Me: Character and Temperament Types*, Prometheus Nemesis Book Company, US (1984)

P Kline, *A Handbook of Test Construction*, Methuen (1986)

K M Miller, *Psychological Testing in Personnel Assessment*, Gower Press (1975)

Isobel Myers and Peter Myers, *Gifts Differing*, Consulting Psychologists Press, US (1988)

Brian O'Neill, *The Manager as an Assessor: A Manager's Guide to Assessing and Selecting People*, The Industrial Society (1990)

Boris Semeonoff, *Personality Assessment*, Penguin (1966)

M Smith et al, *Selection and Assessment: A New Appraisal*, Pitman (1989)

C G Thornton and W C Byham, *Assessment Centres and Managerial Performance*, Academic Press, US (1982)

Leona E Tyler, *Tests on Measurements*, Prentice Hall, US (1963)

Specific tests

H J Eysenck, *Know Your Own IQ*, Penguin (1962)

Anna Freud, *The Ego and the Mechanisms of Defence*, The Hogarth Press (1976)

Ulf Kragh and Gudmund Smith, *Precept Genetic Analysis*, Gleerups Lund, Sweden (1970)

Herbert Phillipson, *The Object Relations Technique*, Tavistock Publications (1955)

Bill Reddin, *Tests for the Output Oriented Manager*, Kogan Page (1991)

Team testing

R M Belbin, *Management Teams: Why They Succeed or Fail*, Heinemann (1981)

P Ramsden, *Top Team Planning*, Cassel (1973)

M Woodcock, *Team Development Manual*, Gower Press (1979)

See also the following journals:

The Journal of Applied Psychology
Personnel Psychology
Psychological Bulletin
Guidance and Assessment Review
Personnel Management
Journal of Occupational Psychology
Bulletin of the British Psychological Society

Index